Bridges, Paths, and Waters;
Dirt, Sky, and Mountains

Bridges, Paths, and Waters; Dirt, Sky, and Mountains

A Portable Guided Retreat on Creation, Awe, Wonder, and Radical Amazement

N. Thomas Johnson-Medland

RESOURCE *Publications* • Eugene, Oregon

BRIDGES, PATHS, AND WATERS; DIRT, SKY, AND MOUNTAINS
A Portable Guided Retreat on Creation, Awe, Wonder, and Radical Amazement

Copyright © 2010 N. Thomas Johnson-Medland. All rights reserved. Except for brief quotations in critical publications or reviews, no part of this book may be reproduced in any manner without prior written permission from the publisher. Write: Permissions, Wipf and Stock Publishers, 199 W. 8th Ave., Suite 3, Eugene, OR 97401.

Resource Publications
An Imprint of Wipf and Stock Publishers
199 W. 8th Ave., Suite 3
Eugene, OR 97401
www.wipfandstock.com

ISBN 13: 978-1-60899-556-1

Manufactured in the U.S.A.

All scripture quotations, unless otherwise indicated, are taken from the Holy Bible, New International Version®, NIV®. Copyright ©1973, 1978, 1984 by Biblica, Inc.™ Used by permission of Zondervan. All rights reserved worldwide.

This book is dedicated to Glinda, Zachary and Josiah—my family. They love God, nature, and campfires with a zeal that keeps me fresh. And, to all of the campers, counselors, volunteers, and staff of the Pocono Plateau Camp and Retreat Center.

It is those we live with and love and should know who elude us. Now, nearly all those I loved and did not understand when I was young are dead, but I still reach out to them.

Of course, now I am too old to be much of a fisherman, and now of course I usually fish the big waters alone, although some friends think I shouldn't. Like many fly fisherman in western Montana where the summer days are almost Arctic like in length, I often do not start fishing until the cool of the evening. Then in the Arctic half-light of the canyon, all existence fades to a being with my soul and memories and the sound of the Big Blackfoot River and a four-count rhythm and the hope that fish will rise.

Eventually, all things merge into one, and a river runs through it. The river is cut by the world's great flood and runs over rocks from the basement of time. On some of the rocks are timeless raindrops. Under the rocks are the words, and some of the words are theirs.

I am haunted by rivers.

—Norman Maclean
"A River Runs Through It"

Preface

HOW TO USE THIS MANUAL

With the exception of the introduction—which simply sets the scene and gives definition and direction to the rest of the work—this manual is broken down into small bite size modules for pondering, meditating, and responding. Each module reflects the same structure as the one before it. The content will be different and the focus will be unique.

I suggest you invest in the process by allowing yourself 20—30 minutes to sit with the material presented and then respond to it. The work here is one of seeing, feeling, and connecting. It is the work of interacting with stimulus and recognizing how it affects us within. It is the process that goes on in creating any great piece of art.

The work in each section revolves around a nature poem. Read it. Re-read it and then gather some focusing words from the discussion immediately following the poem. The discussion is meant to draw out some ideas and impressions that are left with us on reading the poem. The discussion will help us to find some ways in which the words have stirred things within us as well.

After the discussion there will be space to interact with some questions. This interaction is really how spiritual direction and formation is done. Good "Spiritual Direction and Formation" is nothing more than offering the seeker relevant questions to mull over. Through interaction we muddle around and give voice to unnamable things we are feeling and to hidden ways we are connecting with the words of the poem. You will be creating your own piece of art—through your interior interactions with the poems—that reflects your wanderings amid the topics presented.

Read the poem one more time before you begin to interact with the questions.

Because it is a spiritual retreat, you may be inclined to think of your responses as something other than art. But, they are your internal creations. A spiritual retreat helps us to create—within and around us—the life that we believe we are "called to" and "asked" to live. We are creating and that is art.

Find yourself a space that is conducive to silence and wonder. A spot by a lake, by a tree, or perhaps in your backyard. If you cannot find these things, then finding a piece of art or an object of nature that represents these things is fine. Find an awesome and magnificent view and prepare yourself to create anew the life you have been given—one breath and one day at a time.

The ideal setting would be for you to go away, to a retreat house, in the "wilds". Spend time slowly walking and breathing in the air of the place. Take simple meals. Observe silence. Share this time with a few friends or go it alone. Maybe there is a family cabin, if there is no retreat house; or a friend's vacation home on the beach or in the woods.

The journey of retreating is an age-old form of direction and formation. The silence and the focus allow us to uncover things that we may never have the chance to notice in our everyday lives. The questions give us pause to make connections and discoveries that we may easily miss in our routines. Go to your retreat and to your heart and wander.

Acknowledgments

I WANT TO THANK all of the readers who helped me wrestle with the content in this book. They helped me to clarify meaning, add value, and chase the trail that leads to better writing. Thanks to Mark Robbins, PhD and Glenn Walsh, MAH lifelong friends that gave me immense support and guidance in this book and in all of life. Thanks also to two members of the Order of Saint Luke who provided supportive words and prayers to the text and my spiritual journey: Brother John Dornheim and Sister Lucy Porter.

Introduction

THERE IS SOMETHING HAUNTING about water. There is a power in her to lure and lull us. It is not just her power to drown or destroy. She holds silent things within. There is a lot of silence in her, and a lot of aged knowledge from seeing and passing all that has been. That is her wisdom. That silence is her power.

Rivers have seen passages of time that we can only guess at or imagine. Rivers wrap themselves over the planet in space, but have existed like this over time.

Her wisdom spans through time and is held treasure within her very being. Perhaps she can answer the thunderous questions of the Holy One that were hurled at Job in chapter 38 (verses 19–33). Questions about where the abode of light is hidden. Questions about where the rain and the hail come from and who parents them. Questions that challenge our small understanding and insignificant status on this earth-place we call home.

The water of the rivers, streams, and oceans may have answers to these questions that we have no right guessing at in our short life spans. Perhaps all that they have seen and witnessed has been absorbed into each cell of every drop of the earth's waters. There is something about water that makes us calm. Water exudes a peace that can only come from wisdom. It may be that this peace comes from the wisdom of knowing that everything shall pass, that everything will move on and become something else.

I believe that bridges and paths hold much of the same. There is a silence in them, too. There is an aged knowledge and wisdom in them that is built up over time and space, too. It is the same with dirt, and sky, and mountains. Their silence harbors testimony to the mysteries of creation and the beauty of created and dappled things. They own a deepness that may not be named, but may clearly be felt.

I have often pondered beside these features in our world; and pondered about them. I have sat for hours on end staring at them and surrounding their essence with my "self"; and surrounding my "self" with them. I have put my feeling into them and pulled them back into me. I have reached out to feel what it is to be a bridge, a path, water, dirt, sky, or a mountain. I have imagined their place in my life—in our lives.

There is an overarching depth to their individual presence. There is an abysmal stillness to them that calls us out of ourselves into the open. Hidden in the apparent motionlessness of each is the ability to move things. Whether carrying things on her back, along her banks, like a river or the enabling of simple passage—one side to another—one place to another like a path or bridge, the object that seems so sure and immovable facilitates movement.

Things that appear to be still like this are in constant motion. It may only be the motion of slow and steady growth, or of the terrestrial turning on an axis, but things that appear still are moving. T.S. Eliot writes about it as a still point that exists at the center of things that are turning. Though this appears to be the other side of the conversation about all things moving, it brings us around full circle. There is stillness in motion and motion in stillness.

This conundrum drawls out my interest. These images elicit my adoration and awe. A place of such motion is a place of utter stillness. It is odd; stillness and motion being in the same place at once. As with other conundrums—such as an echoing silence or a grand humility—time and space are spanned with little care for resolution and closure.

With dirt, sky, and mountain the riddle is no different. Each appears to be stoically still and immovable, but the changes of weather and time move them all about. The seasons move across and through them and alter their shape and place—removing any true sense of stillness. Time and space converge and transport all things beyond what they merely appear to be. That is the depth all things have. Perhaps one of the mysteries of creation itself is that things are more than they appear.

There is another sense that draws me out. It is the sense that these things mirror or image deeper more majestic truths in us. They speak to us about who we are. Paths and waters start at a point far away; a place we cannot see. They move away from that unseen place and move closer to us—to our seen place.

Moving from the invisible to the visible is a pattern I notice in my interior life and the lives of those I know. Feelings and responses emerge from within us and we are not able to trace their winding banks to discover their origins—not at first. As time goes on and we trace their path we may find out just where they come from and what gives them birth.

The dirt, sky, and mountains are no different. They exhibit this characteristic depth. They mirror our lives in some way. When we look at these wonders of God, a line is drawn out from our eyes to a point of observation in one of these—our sisters of creation. We connect with things outside of ourselves. We sense an "us-ness" to creation and at the same time a "not-usness". It is at once familiar yet unknown.

The process is not complete. Somehow, something in these sisters of creation undauntingly elicits a spark of awe, wonder, and radical amazement. Somehow, in the relationship of discovery we find a familiarity and a respect. The beauty of these objects of nature triggers a line to be drawn back to us. This one goes right into our heart and causes us to shudder meeting our soul on the way. How did that start? Who parented that notion? What is the abode of that thought? Like Job, we stand aghast. Not only do we connect with things, but also we somehow bring them consumptively back into ourselves.

All this talk of where things came from reminds me of our notions about the origins of space and time. Our best guesses and our most ancient myths try to piece together how we have come out of the unseen; how things emerge out of nothingness. It is the "mysterium tremendum" of Rudolf Otto, a great mystery wrapped up in numinous dread, awe, and awe-fullness—something immense coming out of the darkness.

This great mystery is our depths crying out to the depths of all we experience in an attempt to gain some insight from the echoes of our crying. We yearn and long into space and time. We weave tales we imagine to be true from what we think we sense. We desire for meaning and answers in every step and every moment. Nature plays the role of the great object in the of echolocation of being. Perhaps nature looks to us for the same.

We create stories about immense views of beauty and vistas of glory. We try to make sense out of the rapture we feel when in the presence of mystery. All of that "making sense" is of lesser value than the moment of wonder itself. It dilutes wonder. We want to know what we have to offer each other in this relationship called life. We try to put this into words and then unpack the words for slogans we can repeat, small little morsels we can hold onto.

This great mystery begs the questions wrapped around the big bang or the point of creation as an idea. This mystery of things moving out and away from their point of origin, moving toward us and becoming more visible, more solid, creates the question, "If we go back, do we eventually see all things merging into one? Behind that, is the VOID at this place?" Is their a place from which God uttered all things into being, a still small place hidden in time? Is there an alpha point, an omega point?

What if we go back to the moment before the WORD is uttered at creation. Before anything emerges from the darkness, would we see a pre-eternal oneness of all that is? Is there a visible, conjoined something? Or, is the very question ridiculous because there would be no matter created to be visible and so there could be no seeing?

These are the sorts of begging our heart does in the face of grandeur and beauty and silence. When we stand before a mountain, our soul cries out "Tell me about how things are". As we stand in quiet stillness observing the view, everything in us is in motion for an answer. Everything within is reaching out from us. We call this dense mass of paralyzing feeling "awe".

Awe is a unique creature. It has sisters. Abraham Joshua Heschel has named her sisters "wonder", and "radical amazement" (Man is Not Alone—Farrar, Strauss, Giroux). Matthew the Poor called this territory "ecstasy"—from the Greek Fathers' teachings on "ekstasis" (Orthodox Prayer Life—Saint Vladimir's Press). However we call it, it is that overwhelming feeling in the heart, that immense presence in the soul that makes us feel so infinitesimally small (dwarfed by the view of the Grand Canyon or the Pleiades) that we feel immense (somehow at one with the Spirit, or all creation). Here is another riddle. Called into smallness, we become grand.

This conundrum of being tiny enough to be everything is exactly what makes awe such a transforming gift of the Spirit. The poems of Rumi are full of this "noticing" of awe that pushes people into union with the Creative Father. Someone may be sitting at a table drinking tea and the note of a flute hits them and awakens them to some hidden mystery. Someone walking down a path may see a rose and all of the sudden—in an instant—everything they have been living "makes sense" for just a second. These flashes of understanding are wrapped-up in awe and they are "Gifts of the Spirit" and they call us into union with the Divine Father.

Nature too lures us into this divine trap. As an instrument of the Spirit, creation beseeches us to look and interact. We start to ponder and to surmise, the next thing we know we are overwhelmed by the depth of creation and snared by the idea that we stand as nothingness against the grand scheme. Mystery subsides and a sense of union and connectedness arises. We feel at one with all God has done. We are lulled into this place against all reason. We are often brought into our heart against our mind's wishes to figure it all out.

The lives of the mystics were really lives of learning to cope with this awe. The scent of a flower on the wind took our brother Francis of Assisi to great heights of ecstasy in the Merciful One. The sight of a sunrise moved our sister Theresa to feel connected with the Creator. The sound of the rushing falls—over the rocks and into the pools—lured Hildegard into being lost in the great ground of our being.

Awe, ecstasy, wonder, and amazement make us small enough that we can carry the One who is Uncircumscribable. That is the power afoot here. When we become small; then we are large. When we are weak; then we are strong. When we disappear; then HE appears. "All is perishing—except His Face" (the Koran 28:88).

What follows are words and poems that reveal stillness and motion, movement from and toward, passage through space and time. They are descriptions of awe, beauty, wonder, glory, and radical amazement. These can only give a hint at or point toward the actual experience of these things. Once we realize what they are hinting at or pointing to, then we are undone. Once we are onto the scent, or uncover the trail we are no good for this world. We are set loose in an encounter with the Living God of all creation; an encounter in which we lose ourselves to our Beloved.

Capturing the illusory nature of life and its images is as fleeting as grasping at mist, and yet in the activity of trying to make out what is before us and all around us we do find a few laconic and lapidary images that will make themselves into agents of rapture and amazement. We all find a few pearls of wisdom to help carry us through our days on this earth place. We are awakened a few times to the infinite glory by the stuff all around us.

These things, these things that we try to figure out and these things that we invest with meaning; it is these things that we can only hope to discover. If we find any of them in this one lifetime, we are home. We will have arrived. The arduous task of living has these words to offer: "Do not ever lose your ability to be moved by a sunrise. Do not ever stop crying when you see the ocean. Feel the wind blow through you. Be opened up by everything you experience." We must be always interacting with the stuff of life. We must walk away from these encounters deeper people. These encounters are what nature call us into.

If we find out what it means to be a bridge, or a path, or water, to be dirt, and sky, and mountain, then we find out a piece of our own "selves". For, surely, we are not only "apart from" the things around us, but we are "a part of" the things around us. All about us are things that inform us about how life is and who we are.

One of the powers of poetry is that it evokes immense and varied images. It evokes ideas and feelings that are vast and seemingly unrelated or conflictual. As we look at these images and discuss them, it is important to recognize that we may come up against things that seem to be broken or in opposition to something else inside of us. We may be left feeling we have not resolved something. Poems may unearth some deep mystery within us. Poems set us on the path of mystery and connection.

Our work with nature and awe should teach us that we are standing in the face of something we cannot wrap our intellect around fully. We feel tiny and unimpressive next to this great scene, vista, or moment, and yet at peace and one.

Contemplating nature can be disturbing. When we unearth unsettling impressions from within ourselves, we are just finding something new that we have not been able to wrap our mind around. We are standing in the presence of a mystery. Some mysteries become revealed. Other mysteries stay mysterious. We are able to express some things that we encounter, other things we can only sense.

There are moments in our lives that we see this same beauty in other people. We sense the depth and the stillness that they exude. We are in awe of someone else. We ourselves may become objects of awe to other people. We see a hungry man offer a cold man his coat. A mother awakens repeatedly to feed her son. A woman holds the hand of her dying sister—and sings. As in nature, we often come upon great vistas in the lives of our brothers and sisters. They are as vast as the dirt, the sky, and the mountains. Rivers are not the only sisters of creation that lull us into union with God.

There is a wonderful quote from Shantideva's "Guide to the Bodhisattva's Way of Life" (Shambala Press, Boston, MA, 2006) that reads: "May I be a protector for those without one, a guide for all travelers on the way; may I be a bridge, a boat, and a ship for all who wish to cross the water."

This quote sets out a way in which we may be the still motion for others. We may be an object that helps move folks from one place to the next. We may be a vessel for those who need transport. We may help our own selves move from one place to another on the spiritual journey called life, called faith.

The Father of all may call us to move others along the way. We must allow ourselves the grace of being a depth and stillness that others aspire toward as well. Just as we have already ascribed to the natural world of creation, we ourselves maybe a part of the process of union that others go through.

These terrains we cross, they are always changing. At one place in life, we may ford the rivers of pride; at another we may cross on the bridge of desire. Some days we cross the desert of apathy, others we search for the path of kindness that climbs through the hills. Others journey the same as we do. They encounter the same terrain. They look to us for meaning and understanding. We ourselves may be the object of the echolocation of being for another.

We ourselves—as Shantideva proclaims for us—can be vehicles to support others through their journey. As caring people who lend aid to other travelers throughout life we must remain flexible, available, and open. If we do not we may not be of service. We must be pliable enough to hearken unto the voice of the Spirit and compassionate enough to be the exact vehicle needed—these are tricky balances to maintain.

Can there be anything more useless and more "in your face" than the wrong vehicle in the wrong place. If a person needs a path across a hot desert, being a boat will be of no use. If a log bridge is needed to cross a stream, being a path will be useless. What sense does it make to see a rowboat in the middle of the desert? What good is the path if you are trying to get across the stream to the other bank?

Being compassionate requires suppleness and discernment. We must ferret out the need and be able to adapt our "selves" to the task at hand. This can only be done with the Spirit; and the terrain of the Spirit, the vehicle of the Spirit is the same: THE HEART. If you are all about living in the Spirit of God, and you are living outside of the HEART, than you probably are not where you think you are. Or, at the very least, you are using the wrong vehicle to get there. The life of the Spirit is the life of the HEART. If you do not know what that means, then the journey has just begun.

Nature becomes our partner not only in the deepening of our own individual selves, but in the process of helping others to deepen as well. We are a all a part of creation. Therefore, the connection to our world is deeper than just self worth. It is about wholeness—the wholeness of all that is.

As we embark on this great journey of faith, focusing in this retreat on the depth and motion of creation in our lives, let us never forget our place in it. We are a part of all that has been brought forth by God. It is not only the ocean that is deep, but our brother is deep as well. It is not only the river that comes toward us from an unseen place, but our feelings as well. It is not only the earth that shifts and slides as an escarpment is being born, but our hearts as well. We are, as John Donne proclaimed, pieces of the whole.

May the poems and the exercises that follow lead you to a place of wonder, and awe, and radical amazement—a place that lulls you into union with our Imaginative Father and all that He has summoned from His WORD.

1

POEM

"River Bending"

We are not here
long enough
to watch the river
change her shape.
But she does.
I have felt it.
We can see her swell
and dry, but we do
not get to see her
curl and cut and
grow old. She is an
old thing. She goes
back a thousand,
thousand years.
We cannot see all the
changes, but we can
feel them. They are
in there.

DISCUSSION

The natural world or creation may often bear witness to many more things than we are able to. Creation has seen everything that has happened. The rivers have been around so long that they have seen struggles we have had upon this land. They have seen the overthrowing of the Indian nations, and the battles against the Crown, the war that divided the states against each other, and the pioneering of outer space.

Think of all that has gone on from the dawn of time, from the beginning of creation. There are members of the natural world who have seen things of which we can only dream. This should change how we view ourselves in relation to time, and space. We have been here for only a short time. We have seen only a fraction of history unfold.

There are people in our lives who may also have a broader and more complete view of time and space. This is not only because of the number of their days here on this earth. It is also because of the number and types of experiences they have had while here on this earth.

What this gets at is that no man is an island. We need others to make sense out of the "whole picture of life". Pieces of how life is may not be at our disposal to understand, interpret, or even postulate. Pieces of life's history are only known to the ancient ones. Those ancient ones are the mountains, the trees, and the rivers.

We depend on geological records to help us see what has happened on the earth through time. We check for fissures and fossils to help us understand what the earth was like thousands of years ago. We look for petrification and erosion to mark time.

We need to depend on human elders to help us interpret the flow of history. We need older citizens to understand that the social enormity of the Great Depression was not just financial, but ethical, and spiritual, too. They need to tell us how it sapped peoples' ability to make good decisions and hold out for hope.

A river changes shape over time. Erosion and flooding alter the course of her banks. Rivers grow from side-winding snake-like shapes to straightened shortcuts that bypass the turns of time. Rivers meander and overflow. The changes all take place over time and are the result of forces imposed on the river. That is not so different from how we are changed and become changed ourselves.

Some days we are willing to go through the winding and ambling nature of life. We are unafraid to meander and side-wind from one phase to the next. Taking twists, turns, and lengthy forays does not bother us. However, there are other times in life when we want a shortcut. We will take a straight, direct, and overpowering direction in order to get from "a" to "b". We over flow our banks and dissect the normal flow of life and change.

When you see a river from above you often are able to see the riverbeds that have been there in the past. You can see how in the glacial changes of time the river was much larger or had a different shape and course. All of this comes from having a vantage point, a place to see from—to interpret from—that allows you a broad view. Vantage points are revealing.

Standing on hills, or bridges, or mountains, above the terrain, gives us an inner feeling of vision and fullness. Many times, we may have a startling revelation of how a river really flows when we see it from a higher vantage point. We may say, "I never knew those two villages were so close before." Or, "It is no wonder that place floods, it is a perfect spot for a rushing river to shortcut its winding banks." Or, "Look, you can see where the loops of the side-winding have built up with silt over the years of flooding."

There are times in our lives when we feel as if we have arrived at a vantage point. We find some small vision into how our lives have been that seems to unfold countless maps of meaning—and we suddenly make sense out of something we could not grasp. When we grasp it, we can feel it in our center in a way that only makes sense when we think of viewing some natural marvel. This revelation becomes awe-inspiring.

The feelings we get at these moments of revelation are felt in the center of the chest. We connect with something larger than ourselves in such a way as to understand it in our head, but feel it viscerally in our chests and in our guts.

When we begin to take these lessons away from creation, we begin to recognize how it is truly a partner with us in this life. It is not necessarily something we are here to rail against or whip into shape. Nature is a valuable extension of our own life—a piece of the whole.

It is important for people to be able to plug into these larger and somewhat expansive feelings. The feelings that come from standing at the Grand Canyon or on a vantage point viewing a river. It opens in us a perspective that reminds us of our place in the whole. It also opens in us a silence that reveres. Standing in wonder at the grandeur of life and the Creator allows us to expand beyond the boundaries of our daily self.

GLEANINGS

Pearls of Wisdom we have found in this poem:

- ❖ Time changes things
- ❖ Seeking a vantage point can help us understand
- ❖ We can feel change as well as know it
- ❖ Change alters us in many ways
- ❖ There is an inner wisdom that comes from aging and changing over time
- ❖
- ❖
- ❖
- ❖
- ❖
- ❖
- ❖
- ❖
- ❖
- ❖
- ❖
- ❖
- ❖

INSIGHTS

What leaps out at you from the poem:

What descriptive words do you like or identify with:

What colors, moods, or emotions do you hear in the poem:

What spiritual value or trait do you overhear in these words:

How does the HOLY ONE fit into this imagery or notion:

6 BRIDGES, PATHS, AND WATERS; DIRT, SKY, AND MOUNTAINS

How would you change or enrich the poem:

Write your own poem or paragraph of prose to encapsulate similar ideas:

How does the HOLY ONE speak to you through these ideas:

How do you feel your life being called to change:

Is there someone you feel would connect with the ideas in this poem:

Pretend you were writing to that person (above), how would you describe what you have learned or felt to them:

8   BRIDGES, PATHS, AND WATERS; DIRT, SKY, AND MOUNTAINS

Draw this poem:

How does this connect you to awe, wonder, or radical amazement:

2

POEM

"Simply Heather"

Looking through the heather
the heart of the mountain
turns to azure cool depths
and pools of water.
Climbing stone on stone
moss wraps its limbs
around moist hardness.
A wind sails over the whiskers
of a seal sleeping on a pile
of seaweed. Why are we so
determined to remove ourselves
from this feeling of awe that
surrounds us in the wilds. I could
write these lines again and again.
The ocean comes in to lick the
shore, and we are embarrassed.
The sun screams out beauty in
its descending pinks and oranges,
and we cover our ears. Why do we
complicate the beautiful array of
mismatched and untied strings
by tying odd ends together?

DISCUSSION

There is a rawness to the experience of grandeur and beauty in nature. We are swept away by how it looks. How it reaches into our chest and belly and makes us feel small and yet connected. It is a sensual experience. It involves the fullness of our senses.

You get this understanding when you are in the center of an experience of awe. Somehow, you feel a part of the scene you are looking at. There is a reaching out from your center to the object and a reaching into your center from the object. An expansive vista grabs hold of you. A mountain makes you infinitesimally small. You reach out from within to make some sort of connection.

It is really something that cannot be put into words. It is ineffable. That is what makes it an "awesome" experience. It is experienced. It is lived in the center of our bodily real estate—in us.

Hearken back to the words of the author of the "Tao Te Ching". The text essentially starts by saying, "the Tao that can be named is not the limitless/eternal Tao". There is a real acknowledgement in wisdom literature that you cannot put words to a rapturous experience in such a way so-as-to carry the full "rapturousness" of the experience. Words diminish the experience.

The fullness is in the experience itself. It fades when it is brought further away from the experience either by time or by words. A painting is somehow less than the scene it depicts. In the absence of the experience itself we craft words to describe, inform, and hedge in what it is we remember of what we had experienced.

You can only approach the thing. You can only get close to carrying the full measure of import, but not "actually". Many have said, "How can you describe the taste of the saltiness in the ocean?"

When you stand and see the heather, or the pool of water you can reach out into it with your heart and with your soul. You can swim around in it. You can even write about it, but there is something different about the words used to surround the experience with definition and the actual living out of the definition by experience.

The best we can hope for is that the words will somehow carry enough symbolism or meaningful, verbal nano-technology to recreate the experience. Even though the experience may be recreated, it is never the exact same. The recreation may be close, but experiences fade into history with ease.

When our eyes help our heart and soul to go out of ourselves and onto the rock or through the whiskers of the seal, we pause for a moment and feel it. Staying with that feeling and that moment is a gift. It may perhaps seep and saturate into another moment. And, perhaps even into a third moment—feeling like all eternity. The rareness of this gift of experience and awareness is novel and we often leave it, quickly moving on because of the immensity of the feeling. To hold and stay in the grandeur of that moment is more than a gift. It is a skillful art. It is an art that should be practiced more often.

There is a discomfort that comes after soaking in so much hugeness and so much connection. We can feel small, and in awe, and connected to a mountain, a ravine, and an oceanic vista, but only for so long before we feel the need to exert our independence and claim "I am not this".

So goes the dance of union. We reach out, we connect, and we retreat again into our tiny-ness. It is the rhythm of how we relate, how we bond, and how we attach. We do it in friendships, in projects, and in experiencing.

What is wonderful is that we can teach ourselves to expand our time of union. We can stay with a vista a few more minutes. We can stand in awe just a few more seconds. We can bond for ten minutes longer. It takes practice.

Part of the pulling away is done so that we can put a name to what we are feeling. It somehow undoes us to have no words for an experience. We need to be able to have some kind of impact on the thing itself, so we name it, define it, and put it on some sort of logical shelf. We try to contain what is uncontainable. We wish to share it.

To allow the realm of the world to saturate us without any type of explanation is not only expanding, but it opens us to more of life and it satisfies some "ancient lurking passion" to be a part of something larger than ourselves; to be a part of everything. It is critical to our human interior health to be cut loose into the bigness-of-life-that-is-not-us.

This goes on all of the time. We look at scenes outside of ourselves and bring them back inside to feel them and to interpret them. Just like things we cannot see, we would not know this is happening unless we saw the process happening from a distance. The distance may be a result of time (like reading about our experiences in a journal) or a result of space (like seeing the process unfold in someone else). This is why language has become so critical to people. It provides space to gain a vantage point on our own lives.

GLEANINGS

Pearls of Wisdom we have found in this poem:

- ❖ We can connect with what we see

- ❖ Things around us have a heart or center

- ❖ Awe helps us to connect with things larger than us

- ❖ Wonder helps us to feel a part of larger things

- ❖ We often retreat from large feelings of connectedness and intimacy

- ❖ We can put words to something and not have them really explain the thing itself

- ❖ Trying to tie things up nicely is not always necessary

- ❖
- ❖
- ❖
- ❖
- ❖
- ❖
- ❖
- ❖
- ❖
- ❖

INSIGHTS

What leaps out at you from the poem:

What descriptive words do you like or identify with:

What colors, moods, or emotions do you hear in the poem:

What spiritual value or trait do you overhear in these words:

How does the HOLY ONE fit into this imagery or notion:

How would you change or enrich the poem:

Write your own poem or paragraph of prose to encapsulate similar ideas:

How does the HOLY ONE speak to you through these ideas:

How do you feel your life being called to change:

Is there someone you feel would connect with the ideas in this poem:

BRIDGES, PATHS, AND WATERS; DIRT, SKY, AND MOUNTAINS

Pretend you were writing to that person (above), how would describe what you have learned or felt to them:

Draw this poem:

18 BRIDGES, PATHS, AND WATERS; DIRT, SKY, AND MOUNTAINS

How does this connect you to awe, wonder, or radical amazement:

3

POEM

"A Coldness"

I reach down deep in the dirt
and there is a coldness.
Not the coldness of being rude,
but the coldness of rugged surviving.
Surviving against all odds;
surviving in the face of a
fierce and mighty foe.
Thistles grow like this.
Heather grows like this.
In the face of death,
some people grow like this -
grow towards deep
strength and coldness.
Standing on the edge
of the waters
the purple and the mist are
a ways off. They lift
me up and bolster me
from my heart.

Seals and gulls flop
and poke themselves
through the seaweed,
looking for treasures
and for things to do.
They are toughened by this.

They have saved themselves for
life and for death—being able
to play. They have saved themselves
from building bridges, and roads
and nuclear reactors.

They all slip, back into the cold,
surviving against all odds, against
the desire to overdo and subdue.
Against the desire to create monstrous
chaos that they will become unable
to live without. And soon, unable to live
with. They slip through the golden
weeds, soaked with wet chill cold, and
are gone.

DISCUSSION

There are periods in life when we feel hemmed in or hedged about by the need to simply survive. These are the days without frills or fanfare. We do not do anything extra during this time—either by choice or by necessity. These periods are Lenten in their nature, filled with abstaining and a sense of fasting.

Like the heather or the thistle these times are lean survivor-times. Little nourishment is taken in but life is expected to be sustained. Nutrients are to be grabbed from thin air.

For the most part, we may not recognize that we are heading into such a time, or that we are in such a time. We may only recognize that we do not feel quite right, or that we notice a scarcity of resources, or we have tightened our belts after the time of surviving is over. Many times we are emotionally distant, inattentive, or unable to focus in these dire and sparse times.

If we find ourselves in the middle of a period of wanting, it is good medicine for us to practice the art of play. We should set aside time to do something silly and meaningless because the rest of our days seems dour. Offsetting the emptiness of need with the abundance of recreation can nourish us. It is a chance to focus more deeply upon what we already have—relationships and character.

I think back to times of tragedy. When there have been great losses or death, I have needed to enter a dry spell, a period of less. Clearly these were times of taking stock. They were times of measuring quality. These times can actually be a period of healing—making do with less, but recognizing how vital that little bit we have truly is.. This means less emotion, less activity, and even less thought.

This lightening of the load is similar to entering into winter. There is less light, we end up hunkering down, our mobility is stifled. We may turn our attention to the quality of the interactions we do have—a deepening element of play. We move more slowly to sustain what we have, to conserve our resources toward the future.

All around us, nature gives us examples of what this time looks like. Rivers and lakes freeze over. Fish and water life settle motionless to the bottom. Life seems to stand still. Animals disappear. The air becomes still and the sky gets heavy. Things are heading into hibernation. A deepening rest of lessening is coming upon us.

This is what St. John called the" dark night of the soul". It is a critical period of downtime in which nutrients are systematically drawn out of everything around so that life can go on. Movement and growth appear to be minimal, but life is sustained. Whole portions of our "self" may migrate to warmer climates, while others settle in for the winter.

Thistles, heather, seals, and gulls are great images of surviving amid the hunkering down. They seem to need so little to survive. The can thrive on minimal amounts.

I think all of us clearly remember days when we have gotten by with little. We get little emotional, spiritual, physical, or mental input. We made it—survived—on far less than we required at other times.

These days are pure examples of ruggedness. They remind us how truly versatile we are. They are reminders of heliotropes. We like flowers and plants turn toward the sun. We seek out and find life, wherever it may be. We draw nourishment seemingly from thin air.

The notion of hibernation and winter sleep is helpful in connecting to the image in the poem. We can go underground or into a dormant state for some time but still be drawing enough nourishment to be sustained and grow. Under the fallen leaves of autumn, whole systems of life are at play, building toward the powerful emergence of new life in Spring.

Like a bear that emerges from the cave after its winter sleep, life emerges, hungry beyond belief but ready to become what is needed. The movement creates a deeper appetite, a mobile force that consumes anything in its sight. When the waiting is over, it is clearly time to stock up on food. The growth comes hard and fast.

No longer discerning, perhaps the way it would when nourishment is balanced and time is not of the essence, life consumes what it needs in great quantities. The time after a chilling slumber is so opposite in nature to that slumber, we clearly seem to change and become something we have not been.

Times of growth follow lean sleep. That lean sleep is necessary.

GLEANINGS

Pearls of Wisdom we have found in this poem

- ❖ Thistle blooms with minimal input
- ❖ Beauty is often able to be revealed in disparate situations
- ❖ Cold is an image of sleep and hibernation
- ❖ Sometimes we do not recognize when we are hibernating
- ❖ Play is important to our health
- ❖
- ❖
- ❖
- ❖
- ❖
- ❖
- ❖
- ❖
- ❖
- ❖
- ❖
- ❖

INSIGHTS

What leaps out at you from the poem:

What descriptive words do you like or identify with:

What colors, moods, or emotions do you hear in the poem:

What spiritual value or trait do you overhear in these words:

How does the HOLY ONE fit into this imagery or notion:

Chapter 3   25

How would you change or enrich the poem:

Write your own poem or paragraph of prose to encapsulate similar ideas:

How does the HOLY ONE speak to you through these ideas:

How do you feel your life being called to change:

Is there someone you feel would connect with the ideas in this poem:

26 BRIDGES, PATHS, AND WATERS; DIRT, SKY, AND MOUNTAINS

Pretend you were writing to that person (above), how would you describe what you have learned or felt to them:

Draw this poem:

28 BRIDGES, PATHS, AND WATERS; DIRT, SKY, AND MOUNTAINS

How does this connect you to awe, wonder, or radical amazement:

4

POEM

"Stones and Moss"

I am captured by the stones.
The way they sit there—
piled and scattered—
in and out of relation
with each other.

The mosses can fold themselves,
if they like,
over the stones,
making mortar of themselves
for mounds of shifting rock.
They hold me, too.

I sit here,
among them,
and am unable to move;
sucking in the sun
and the rain
and the water
and listening to time pass with the moon—
Wondering how it all has
come together.

Have the rocks
and moss themselves
been arranged in such a pattern,

or do I, in my seeing, arrange them
in what appears to be a pattern—
even when scattered loosely
like debris. Do their forms exist in
any real way other than the way
I think I see them.

DISCUSSION

Some fantastic pieces of Celtic literature come from the Anglo-Saxon stock of stories. Many of them—told by bards and scops—are about the skillful Taliesin. Taliesin was believed to be able to shape shift; from a man, to a trout, to a tree, to a leaf, to a brook, and then back into his shape as a man.

If you stare at nature long enough, you do get the sense that your moving from object to object—connecting with each as you go—is nothing more than a shape shifting. And, the shape shifting itself is nothing more than an encounter with a thousand shapes and forms.

So often in our religious lives, we bristle against ideas that we find heretical and nothing more than lies or imaginings. In fact, many of these ideas are simply things we have not allowed ourselves to feel; giving us some understanding that they may mean something other than what we think we first hear.

I do not believe that I can become a trout. I do believe that my sitting on a rock and staring out over the lake can make me feel free. In my feeling of freedom and expansive openness I can imagine myself being a trout and swimming among the rocks on the muddied bottom; rolling on my side occasionally as I turn this way and that.

Maybe this is all that Taliesin meant. Maybe he didn't really mean anything else. Maybe we should allow ourselves the playful distance necessary to feel freedom and feel beauty and stop shutting it out by boxing it up in platitudes and rules all of the time.

How do we fit into all of this? How are we to live among these fair and awesome scenes? What should we do with our time among such awesome grandeur and grace?

A lot of us stare at nature, in a sort of "rapt awe", not really formulating thoughts and ideas, but feeling them and sensing them. A piece of us shoots out of us from our hearts and scatters among the view, grabbing hold and bonding with all that we see. Sort of like a phantasmagoric photo-spirit. Our senses leap out from us to gather information and bring that information back into us.

On some occasions, we feel the view in our chest, almost like the chords of the heart retract and bring the scene into us from the outside. But, like I said, we don't usually put words to this, we just feel it. It is a strong feeling.

Once the connection has been made, we may tend to wander about a bit. We may pull the scene within and be overwhelmed by the beauty of it all. Our minds may engage and try to make sense out of the bond and describe it or give shape to what we feel. We may wonder in the wandering: "Am I that?", "What is that?", or, "are those things somehow related—to each other or to me?" Any of these momentary mental intrusions are only dwarfed by the profundity of the unity that comes from feeling connected.

Lao Tzu, in "The Hua Hu Ching" gives a phrase to this experience by saying that every moment is passing . . . but our mind wants to fix what we observe in one place. The mind cannot exist in the context of unity and connection. It must separate itself from what is seen and ask questions or make statements to exert its separateness. Beauty and nature challenge us to look at ourselves beyond the simple concept of "mind".

What I think is somehow very clever and at the same time interesting, is the fact that many of the questions or statements that the mind is all about juggling have to do with where the "we"—or the "I"—fits into what we see. Even though we know we are out among the scene, we question how it all comes together.

Most of us never allow ourselves the chance to have these deep thoughts, but we must. We must dapple in the absurd and the profound. We must walk into thoughts that are way over our head, we must bathe in the notion of our own puniness. We must do these things because we really are dust in the wind and should not take ourselves so seriously. We are a piece of a whole, not the apex of the unity.

We would do well to become so overwhelmed with the awe of the Cosmocrator that we believe our presence is insignificant. We must also feel that we are a part of that vista over there—in some small way. We would do well to know that we are like the moss covering the rocks; that we have been scattered by the One who scattered the Himalayas across the face of the earth. We should have moments of feeling infinitesimally grand because we are the fleshy creations of the Father of LIGHT. We are the sons and daughters of the Most High.

Without some sort of mystic connection or mythology in our lives and language, we miss the relevance of our interconnectedness. Without a foray into the notion or feeling that we are ONE, we would completely miss the reality that we are responsible for all that is around us by our connection to it. We are in need of being better caretakers of the sacred and beautiful earth, if not because we are it, because we are deeply connected and a part of it.

These things are only attainable by grandeur amid nature and by poetic understanding of life. Merton challenged us by aligning the mystical and poetic experience. He shared that the two are rooted in a contemplative reception and subsequent artful recapitulation. We do not gain this insight by memorizing bible verses or by listening to sermons. We get this by being dwarfed by greatness and recognizing our place in the web of created life.

It is amazing how an instant can turn into minutes, then moments, and then hours. We can look at the moss covering the rock and then feel ourselves becoming small enough to imagine how wet it is as it drapes over the rocks, or smell the earthy-darkness of its roots clotted with dirt. We feel a sense of wonder but then get trapped in the thousand and one possibilities of how we should interpret that wonder or explain that scene.

GLEANINGS

Pearls of Wisdom we have found in this poem

- ❖ We can be captured or mesmerized by things
- ❖ We can be drawn in by things, attracted by them
- ❖ Everything exists in and or out of relation to itself and or other things
- ❖ Sometimes things in life are covered by other things—hidden
- ❖ When things are covered; they are also buffered against other things
- ❖ Time passes with the sun and the moon, and is marked by such
- ❖ We can imagine ourselves out there, among what we see
- ❖
- ❖
- ❖
- ❖
- ❖
- ❖
- ❖
- ❖
- ❖

INSIGHTS

What leaps out at you from the poem:

What descriptive words do you like or identify with:

What colors, moods, or emotions do you hear in the poem:

What spiritual value or trait do you overhear in these words:

How does the HOLY ONE fit into this imagery or notion:

36 BRIDGES, PATHS, AND WATERS; DIRT, SKY, AND MOUNTAINS

How would you change or enrich the poem:

Write your own poem or paragraph of prose to encapsulate similar ideas:

How does the HOLY ONE speak to you through these ideas:

How do you feel your life being called to change:

Is there someone you feel would connect with the ideas in this poem:

Pretend you were writing to that person (above), how would you describe what you have learned or felt to them:

BRIDGES, PATHS, AND WATERS; DIRT, SKY, AND MOUNTAINS

Draw this poem:

How does this connect you to awe, wonder, or radical amazement:

5

POEM

"Windworn"

Those portions of our
lives that disappear.
Folds of flower flesh
turning to paper with
the passage of time.
Those things are the
stuff the wind blows away.

It comes in sometimes,
quickly from its place
beyond the horizon, and
just picks up whatever it
wants. It throws it down
and watches it bounce.
This wind has power. It
can take things from one
place to another. And,
sometimes it makes
things go away.

I think I have felt it carry
away pieces of who I am
moving still pieces of
who I am from here to there.

I am alright with that. Some
of those pieces I never did
like. Some of them I will just
plain miss. All in all, I like
the cleansing power of the wind.

DISCUSSION

Change is a constant part of the natural world. Whether it is the forces of erosion or shifting soil, rain, snow, sunshine, the "simple" passing of time, or wind, nothing really stays the same for very long in the wild. Things are moving from here to there. Things are breaking down and becoming smaller objects.

I admit that some of the changes may seem infinitesimal to us as we peer in on the intricacies of nature, but they are not small to the wild. Each little shift and movement plays its role in the ongoing interconnection and webbing of all life in the wild. The dying of one type of plant means the hibernation or death of a whole species of animals. Eroding earth means slides that may no longer give root to types of trees.

You really get a sense of the interconnection of life when you get down on your belly and look at the countless bug-and-animal-universes that unfold in the substrata of field grass and swamp. There are whole dependencies that go on in the tiny universe, dependencies that we forget if we do not hunker down and look into the grass and into the weeds. A blade of grass may be protection and a sustaining community of ecological dependency for not only microbes, but also bugs.

The wind can change whole nations of animals and the lives they lead. From the fertilization of plant life to the shifting of snowfall, wind can be a player in the arena of change in nature and the environment. It moves things from one place to another. Wind is a change-agent.

I have seen many things blow across the fields. I love to watch lawn chairs blow away. I love watching papers I have dropped blow just out of reach as I try to pick them up—stumbling all the while. There are other things: dry clumps of leaves and decaying plant matter blow, broken off wings of dead birds blow, exfoliation from trees and plants blow—all of them across the fields.

Time lapsed photography of the erosion of a dead animal shows the slow but steady removal of many layers of the animal's life. Outer coats of fur blow away, then layers of skin dry and blow away, and eventually organs weather and wear as the process of time dries out the remains on the woodland floors. All of the pieces of what-used-to-be become what-will-become. Bones and flesh nourish the earth and the new life that will spring from her crust. Wind facilitates this movement that supports new life.

This kind of removal of layers is something that goes on in our lives all of the time. We may not see the changes over the long haul the way others do, but we do feel them. Others can clearly see the things that are sloughed-off of us at regular intervals. They note the changes over time. They see things from their vantage point that we do not see.

There is a tendency to feel that we are being eroded and changing deeply when we compromise and shift away from our own personal values. When we make these adjustments, we feel a sense of defeat and loss. We feel as if a part of us is gone, taken away, or has left. In order to cope with these alterations and intrusions of life we may down play them or minimize them. We may brush them off like chaffing skin. this does not eliminate the fact that compromise erodes us.

I think a real danger comes when we begin to assign value to changes. When we decide that changes are inherently good or bad, we begin to affect the quality of our lives. We assume that we are ourselves good or bad because of these changes being present in our lives. It is a simplistic and rudimentary response to attribute these values to what leaves us in life's process.

I am not advocating for abandoning self-examination in our lives. I am not saying there is no right or wrong that accompanies our days. I am suggesting that we should remember that many of the changes that occur in our lives MUST occur; everything in life changes. There is no real option or choice involved. It may be better for us to begin by noticing change and its implication in our life instead of first assigning value. We tend to cease our interaction with change once we assign the value of good or bad.

It is wise to back away from our lives on occasion; not to be so harsh, and to just allow the changes to come; to view our lives from a vantage point of grace. When we fight so hard on the surface of our lives, we wear ourselves down. Many times we are missing the essential core to who we are. Many times we miss how change fits in to the larger picture of our lives—the larger flow of our growth.

The changes in life do not have to change all of us—the core of our selves. The things that blow away do not have to affect us intensely. These changes may affect pieces of us, but not the whole. Think about it. Does our losing money have to affect our ability to love? Does the rise of gas prices have to make us bitter people?

We do not need to change because the props of life shift and move all about us. Changes may affect us, but we do not always need to shift our being.

This requires a high level of thinking and a deep commitment to a belief that the core of who we are does not need to be affected by life's changes. Nature is a good teacher. Seasons come and seasons go; the appearance of the terrain may be altered from one year to the next, but the earth still goes on. Life itself still goes on.

Watching the shifting and moving of the created world gets us started asking the questions that support deep interaction with the notions of change. What is it that goes away? Who is it that remains? What is it that changes? Who is the un-changeable self?

How do we cope and adapt to changes? Do we let them shake our foundations and crumble our hope and confidence?

I have never seen a lake cease to be a lake because it floods. I have never seen a field give up on itself because the grasses on its surface catch fire and burn. There is a core of being that is immovable and unalterable and we should recognize this so we don't feel that all our life is shifting sand.

What are the core and essential pieces of who we are? What is at the center of who we are? What is at the center of what it means to be human? What does it mean to be spiritual?

GLEANINGS

Pearls of Wisdom we have found in this poem

- ❖ Changes happen all the time
- ❖ Changes may not be either good or bad
- ❖ To be alive means to change
- ❖ Things blow in and out of our lives
- ❖
- ❖
- ❖
- ❖
- ❖
- ❖
- ❖
- ❖
- ❖
- ❖
- ❖
- ❖
- ❖
- ❖

INSIGHTS

What leaps out at you from the poem:

What descriptive words do you like or identify with:

What colors, moods, or emotions do you hear in the poem:

What spiritual value or trait do you overhear in these words:

How does the HOLY ONE fit into this imagery or notion:

Chapter 5   47

How would you change or enrich the poem:

Write your own poem or paragraph of prose to encapsulate similar ideas:

How does the HOLY ONE speak to you through these ideas:

How do you feel your life being called to change:

Is there someone you feel would connect with the ideas in this poem:

48 BRIDGES, PATHS, AND WATERS; DIRT, SKY, AND MOUNTAINS

Pretend you were writing to that person (above), how would you describe what you have learned or felt to them:

Draw this poem:

How does this connect you to awe, wonder, or radical amazement:

6

POEM

"Swan"

Paddled under on the
broken leg of a swan,
I feel your love
deep in my lake.

Hearts entwine and
flop over with the rising
and the falling of the tides.

Muds stir and plants roll
in the murky waters of
my heart, moving to the
rhythm of that broken leg.

And when she comes proudly
from that lake, she stretches her
wing way back, and in its silent
brokenness,
that wing stares
at you, with her eyes and shows
all the wanting and needing behind
that pride. She is in some pain;
some
pain from just sitting.

Her white is stark
against the water.

Serenity now turns with
her in a small tilt of
the neck. She marks my
eyes with a new gaze.
She knows she must leave
and she does.

Into the water,
our tails raised to
the skies, we look,
searching desperately
for the next thing
that will become a part
of us, and then leave again.

Chapter 6

DISCUSSION

There is a small cyclone of water created when a canoe paddle dips into the water, glides along in a stroke, and is pulled back up from the depths. This is the same cyclone created by the paddling under of a swan's webbed foot or any other waterfowl. Watching the energy pull down into the depths can be mesmerizing. It reminds us that there is an "in-ness" to a body of water—there are depths.

The depths of a lake immediately leap out to us and connect with our hearts, betraying the fact that we have a murky interior; a place where things may not be clearly visible, but are vast, and wide and deep beyond measure. The depth of the interior is not completely knowable all at once, but must be explored, felt and sifted through in order to plum its fullness.

The "in-ness" of our lives is vast and often unexplored. Even if we claim to know our interior well, we cannot help but realize when we see the swan paddling its broken leg into the cyclone that the mud and silt from within are kicked up and alter the view and the shape of the bottom. There may be shoals and markers that we can recognize, but there are changes in there as well.

In the current understanding of the sciences and "field theory", we ourselves are a part of all that is going on around us. There is no separation of "us" and "them". Instead, there is a continuum of reality, a connectedness of things.

This connecting with nature that we have been doing in these exercises is really what is already going on. There is a flow between nature and we alleged observers. There is a seamless fabric of life—or "the field"—and all things are connected within it. For us to stand on the edges of life and connect with nature, drawing analogies from her is not just valuable but necessary. It is all a part of the field. The field is the "whole" that we have spoken of.

Looking down on the broken foot and wing of a swan connects us with what is broken. We all share some understanding of incompleteness or woundedness that is revealed when we see it in front of us. We connect with the pain, with the limitations, and also the strength and power that emerges from a lifetime of coping.

As our eyes pull the information in, as our heart feels connected and expanded, we are realizing the openness and power of "the field" of life. The web of existence is seamless and we are in it well. There is only one distinguishing feature in life, perhaps, it is whether you are able to see and acknowledge the universal thread of pain running through all our lives. Either you get it or you do not.

This is actually one of the great powers of awe, wonder, and radical amazement. Awe, wonder, and radical amazement put us in a place of openness and receptivity to the connectedness of all things. When we stand in awe, wonder, or radical amazement we stand with a hole in our center and the Great Spirit—God—is able to come to us, mingle with us, and become wed to us—in our center. When we stand in the presence of grandeur, we are made small enough to feel dependent on the larger forces of life.

Grandeur helps us to be able to cope, deal, and integrate our brokenness. It lets us see that what is broken in us fits into a much larger picture; that it dovetails with other things all around it. Our brokenness is made whole in its ability to be part of something more.

We connect with that in other people and we see it as beautiful, or at least triumphant. We see it in creation and we notice it as determination and fortitude. When we see it in ourselves we only see it as suffering. This coming up against brokenness in the other heals our own brokenness. Seeing suffering in the great field of beings softens us to suffering that may be present in our own life as well.

We can only hold this thought for so long. Before you know it, we forget that our brokenness is part of a larger whole and we return to feeling our woundedness as suffering. It is that way with other great achievements; we sustain victorious emotions and feelings for a short period of time. We move on.

We are always about moving on. There is a need within us to get the next best thing, to move on to another thing, to try something new—something else. We think that this new thing will be different. It will be able to make us feel better, to feel complete, to take this restlessness away.

Restlessness is a part of the condition that makes us wounded. When we connect with the wounded swan, we see in it the harsh reality that a lot of life is like paddling with a broken leg. We feel that aimless paddling in our chest. How will we view our own woundedness? What answers will we allow for our brokenness? Where will we allow the HOLY ONE to touch us in this misery?

It is in love that the resolution of this poem exists. We make a connection that gets paddled under on the brokenness—into the lake. In the depths of the lake is love. Hidden in the mystery of our heart, in the mystery of the lake is love—the only ability to deal with brokenness that we have. It is compassion that stills the awkward cyclone of suffering in our lives—compassion in all its murky confusion.

GLEANINGS

Pearls of Wisdom we have found in this poem:

- ❖ There are deep places in our lives

- ❖ The deep places of our lives are often murky and unclear

- ❖ We are able to look into these areas and begin to understand

- ❖ Things come and go in and out of our lives frequently

- ❖ We are all broken in places

- ❖ Love is a mysterious path that helps us to accept things

- ❖
- ❖
- ❖
- ❖
- ❖
- ❖
- ❖
- ❖
- ❖
- ❖
- ❖

Chapter 6 57

INSIGHTS

What leaps out at you from the poem:

What descriptive words do you like or identify with:

What colors, moods, or emotions do you hear in the poem:

What spiritual value or trait do you overhear in these words:

How does the HOLY ONE fit into this imagery or notion:

58 BRIDGES, PATHS, AND WATERS; DIRT, SKY, AND MOUNTAINS

How would you change or enrich the poem:

Write your own poem or paragraph of prose to encapsulate similar ideas:

How does the HOLY ONE speak to you through these ideas:

How do you feel your life being called to change:

Is there someone you feel would connect with the ideas in this poem:

Pretend you were writing to that person (above), how would you describe what you have learned or felt to them:

BRIDGES, PATHS, AND WATERS; DIRT, SKY, AND MOUNTAINS

Draw this poem:

How does this connect you to awe, wonder, or radical amazement:

7

POEM

"Have You Noticed"

Have you seen how the ice
coats the branches as they hang down
toward the snow covered earth. A
cold wet sheath wraps itself
one raindrop at a time around
the fingers of the tree; slowly freezing
and dragging the tree
dangerously to the dirt
that is covered itself with ice and snow.

Have you heard how the tree talks
between the branches; a clacking
sound of ice and frozen wood
chattering amongst itself to itself
and for all the world to hear. A
whispering of words and ideas and
imaginings passed on from twig
to trunk to those who pass below.

Have you noticed the feeling you
hold in the center of your soul when
you walk outside in a freshly falling
storm of snow. That stillness that is
somehow not just silence and a not
moving, but a hushed heaviness
that is calling you into deeper places
inside your own self, places of the heart.

DISCUSSION

It is amazing how some of the most beautiful things are so fragile. The very shine that comes from the sun glittering on the sheaths of ice that coat branches in winter storms is precarious for the life of the tree and branch. Should too much of it form on the tree, it can drag branches to the ground, tearing whole limbs from trees under the weight of the icy glow.

Too much snow on a branch can do the same thing. I have seen the whole top of the mountain lose branches on most of its trees from a heavy wet snow that fell early in the season. The tree holds, and holds, and holds the snow until its cold, moist heaviness breaks off limbs—big limbs. Beauty sometimes clears house for us. It ravishes away the deadwood in trees.

Looking at the devastation reminds you of how dangerous it is to be inflexible. It seems the graceful branches of the pines limp to the ground quickly under any weight. The springy nature of her limbs causes the snow to fall off. The branches then rise to collect more snow, and dip, and dump once more. This cycle of suppleness saves the pine her branches. The branches that cannot bend surely break.

Noticing these things often takes some doing. We may walk by these activities every day for a week before we make any kind of connection. We tend to connect when the number of broken limbs rises to the point of being unavoidable. Other scenes in nature grab us by their sheer size and magnanimity. Broken branches here and there may not be enough to make us pause.

There is a lesson here. Could we not alter our lives—become flexible enough—to be able to stop and ponder at the smallest and most seemingly insignificant changes? Could we not move slowly enough through life to be moved and informed by everything around us?

I remember living on the edge of the woods during the summers. I was the nature counselor at a summer camp for a decade. I would sleep out under the stars many nights, eat wild herbs and fish I caught, and shake in dark at the shock and awe of thunder in a valley. One of the spiritual practices I took to then was reading from the Book of Tea.

I remember a story emerging from the whole content of the Zen masters I added to my daily reading. One master used to add three or four stones/pebbles into the bottom of his clay pot. When he boiled water for tea, he would listen for the song of the stones as they danced on the bottom of the pot.

I remember thinking, how odd it was that he would be able to hear the stones. Given the volume of noise that comes from living a life, I did not think I would even notice their sound. As I added stones to my pot, cooking over my Coleman stove, I eventually did learn to hear them. It took some practice.

The next phase of that journey was being able to call their sound a song. At first, it was just a clacking. As the days of summer wore on, and as the memory of stones from year to year grew, I eventually began to hear their clacking as singing. In time, clearly over a long period, I was able to hear and understand.

Noticing often takes a lifetime. There are no guarantees we will get it the first time we experience something. We need to set ourselves to the task.

It is no different in trying to hear chattering in the clacking of frozen tree branches. At first, it is clattering and clacking. Over time—days, perhaps years—the clattering and clacking becomes rhythmic and routine enough to become a language. It becomes the sound of the trees speaking.

There is the thing, allowing something to become a rhythm and a routine in our lives tends to produce the familiarity of interpretation. We are able to hear and understand with practice. How beautiful it would be, if we were comfortable enough with life that we could allow all experience to be familiar enough to open us to its presence and its power.

Meaning comes from opening ourselves to something. Meaning is allowed when we open and allow something to mingle with us and affect us.

Nature is something you must be around for a while before you recognize its presence, and then learn to sense what it is saying. Like being able to hear the clacking of stones in the bottom of a pan of boiling water as a song, it takes some doing, some time. Trees talk. Animals talk. Even silence talks.

When you walk about in snowy woods you notice there is a deep calling. It calls you to searching your own depths. It gives you ample space to respond. It beckons you to respond. A snowy woods allows echoes to sound quite loud. In the stifled stillness, the echo often retreats quickly—beyond our notice.

GLEANINGS

Pearls of Wisdom we have found in this poem

- ❖ The beauty of ice on branches is dangerous to the tree
- ❖ It takes a lot to notice things around us and internalize them
- ❖ We hold feelings inside of us that are connected to what we see
- ❖ Stillness is a powerful and healing force
- ❖ Silence accompanies stillness
- ❖
- ❖
- ❖
- ❖
- ❖
- ❖
- ❖
- ❖
- ❖
- ❖
- ❖
- ❖

INSIGHTS

What leaps out at you from the poem:

What descriptive words do you like or identify with:

What colors, moods, or emotions do you hear in the poem:

What spiritual value or trait do you overhear in these words:

How does the HOLY ONE fit into this imagery or notion:

How would you change or enrich the poem:

Write your own poem or paragraph of prose to encapsulate similar ideas:

How does the HOLY ONE speak to you through these ideas:

How do you feel your life being called to change:

Is there someone you feel would connect with the ideas in this poem:

Pretend you were writing to that person (above), how would you describe what you have learned or felt to them:

Draw this poem:

BRIDGES, PATHS, AND WATERS; DIRT, SKY, AND MOUNTAINS

How does this connect you to awe, wonder, or radical amazement:

8

POEM

"On The Mountain"

There is a spot on the mountain,
a line you cross as you climb.
A place where things
become different.
A space made up of change.

Sometimes it has rain above it
and sometimes it has snow.

It is the place where one thing
ends and another begins.
In grown-up words they want me
to call it altitude,

but children
know it better
inside as magic.

It is magic how on one
side of the line you can have rain,
and then
jumping over the line
your arm freezes as the
snowy flakes land
on the dewy wet of rain.

It is the way
a leaf turns yellow
overnight.
There is a spot on the mountain,
there is a place on the mountain,
there is a space on the mountain
where all things
are made again.

DISCUSSION

I am intrigued by the changes that occur, seemingly beyond our notice, all around us in creation. You can see snow falling ten feet from where you stand. You may see this snow while standing in the rain. Two very different things can occur in close proximity to each other. This is not just in nature, but we often see it here more easily.

You can go to bed one night in a quiet summer evening and wake up in the morning hearing a strong autumn wind, seeing that the leaves all around you have turned fiery red or apple golden. You ask yourself, "Were they like this yesterday? Or, did the wind blow in some sudden change, some autumnal paint?"

The beauty of dappled and varied experience amazes me. It helps all of us to gain perspective when we see differences. Often we think differences around us are only there for us to approve or disapprove of—as if our permission must be granted for something to exist; to be real. I think they give us perspective. They show a depth that reveals distinction.

In the visual world alone, difference allows us to gauge depth. We can tell how far away or how close something is by the depth it casts on the full canvas of our sight. The differences in objects reveal placement. Sounds do the same. We can figure out the nearness or farness of a thing because of its sound in relation to our presence.

The other piece of change that gives me pause, is the lack of awareness that it reveals in us. We see the changing leaves and wonder, "When did that happen?" "How did I miss that?" Changes take us by surprise and remind us that we are not always as aware as we think we are. We can always awaken to a bit more of life.

Once I see that first autumn-changing Sassafras, my mind shifts and says, "fall is coming." I think without the startling presence of bright reds and yellows I would miss the subtle changes in light and temperature as well. I might walk right into winter without noticing a thing.

Changes in our lives are the same. My children are growing everyday, every hour of every day. Still, it does not keep me from waking one morning and looking at my two sons and recognizing that they have grown four inches—seemingly in their sleep. We are startled into seeing development.

Approaching middle-life we find the same awakenings. We wake up one morning to suddenly recognize we are balding, stooped, pudgy, and gray. Quite literally, we are taken by surprise. Perhaps we realize we have become rigid and unforgiving. It does not happen all at once, but we seem to recognize that it has happened "all at once".

This awakening is the place on the mountain. It is the magic vortex where one thing becomes another. It is the line that we cross going up the mountain. It is the line that says, "On this side there is rain, and on that side there is snow".

We tend to view these awakenings with a sense of grief, mourning what we see as losing one thing to gain another. "I can not believe I have not noticed this all along." "I have missed this vital truth". I am not always convinced this is enough. It does not honor the transformation that has occurred, the redistribution of energy into a newer form.

Loss somehow implies that we owned the thing in the first place. Feeling loss focuses on "us" and not the change that has awakened us in the first place. It moves us further away from seeing AWAKENING as the vital thing.

Do we own the time that has shifted from youth to old age? Do we even own the life? Do we own the leaves that have shifted from "greening" to "golding"—the process spanning from springtime birth to fall denouement?

It does not simply call into question who owns these things. It raises the question of what is lost. Is something lost in becoming an adult? Is something lost in becoming a fiery red leaf? Is there some energy that is thrown off in the process—a diminishment? In a sealed system of infinity, are not things simply changing form?

This is not to deny loss in the process of time. It is merely to throw some questions at our ideas of time. Loss does occur, but do things really go away? Are they still in there, only changed?

I think of the aging of my faith. There are times I look at my sons and see such vibrant newness and long for the sparks that once warmed my heart. Then, I remember that the changes in my feeling are not less because of the things I have been through, the time I have traveled this earth-place. No, they are deepened and the sparks are now embers that last into the dark night. The sparks have become coals that can be smoored into a pile, resting patiently until the morning fire (Smooring is the collecting of the peat-fire embers into a pile at day's end. The embers are covered over and held until dawn. They are used to start the new day's fire. See the Carmina Gadelica for Celtic smooring prayers.).

The changes all around us challenge us to look at what it is that changes and what it is that does not. Exuberance may become integrity—no less energy—just different. Walking about freely—busy as a bee—may become non-ambulatory watching, a being taken care of instead of providing care. Interacting with these changes instead of merely grieving the losses can enable us to deepen and open to a much more sensitive existence. The intent is not to deny loss, simply to re-envision what is taking place.

I have noticed as a father that one of my greatest tasks is to help my sons wake up to the changes that are all around and in them. To help them see that what is here now will look and be different in a short while. Who they are now may not always look the same on the outside, but may have some continuity within. The movement and changes of the creation we are swimming in are able to awaken this depth in us as well.

There are times I "notice" because a snow drift is ambling along in the wake of the wind and then suddenly drops off. The abruptness of the image is a catalyst for my opening up—awakening. I sense how many relationships have done the same. I feel how portions of my faith have also dropped off suddenly. It allows me to turn within and begin to lob questions at the changes all about. Why did this happen? How has it affected me? Does it change who I am? How have I stayed the same? How have I coped with the shifting and changing? Where have those things gone? Are they still present, only altered?

The changes themselves are calling out to us to be noticed. Whether it is the browning of a blade of grass or the falling of a feather, they seek our interaction. When we do not wake up from our slumber and see the snow falling on the other side of the stream, we have disengaged from a world that is teaming with consciousness and creativity—a world teaming with the voice of the Divine.

The drop offs are screaming to us to engage. They want us to interact with them and set our hearts to wondering. What could be next? What is growing out of this moment? How will all of this be made new? Transformation comes with every spot, place, and space on the mountain. It is magic. It is not simply altitude.

The real loss that occurs is not seeing the changes happening all around us. God calls us into the present to see the pulse of life. We are entwined with that pulse. How can we not be alive?

GLEANINGS

Pearls of Wisdom we have found in this poem

- ❖ There are places of climate change on mountains
- ❖ You cannot see all of the places where changes occur
- ❖ Snow can happen in one place and rain in another—all within our sight
- ❖ Leaves appear to change over night
- ❖ The places of change in our lives have explanations
- ❖ The places of change in our lives feel magical
- ❖
- ❖
- ❖
- ❖
- ❖
- ❖
- ❖
- ❖
- ❖
- ❖
- ❖
- ❖

INSIGHTS

What leaps out at you from the poem:

What descriptive words do you like or identify with:

What colors, moods, or emotions do you hear in the poem:

What spiritual value or trait do you overhear in these words:

How does the HOLY ONE fit into this imagery or notion:

78 BRIDGES, PATHS, AND WATERS; DIRT, SKY, AND MOUNTAINS

How would you change or enrich the poem:

Write your own poem or paragraph of prose to encapsulate similar ideas:

How does the HOLY ONE speak to you through these ideas:

How do you feel your life being called to change:

Is there someone you feel would connect with the ideas in this poem:

Pretend you were writing to that person (above), how would you describe what you have learned or felt to them:

BRIDGES, PATHS, AND WATERS; DIRT, SKY, AND MOUNTAINS

Draw this poem:

How does this connect you to awe, wonder, or radical amazement:

9

POEM

"Again"

I am not sure if it is
because the woods are so vast
that the smallness of awe in
a tiny trout lily blossom is
almost missed. It may just
be that nothing out here -
living in the mountains as
we now do—ever makes much
fanfare about its existence.
A birthing is about as silencing
as a dying—and you could easily
cross paths with either without
setting out to.

But, once you set your eyes on it,
whether it is a bear trail off into
the brush or a blue jay hopping and
pecking bits of broken nuts, the
kaleidoscope of wonder opens up
and you begin to see a thousand,
thousand strands of interest and glory.

How could you have ever lived a day
without having noticed what a bear
smells like and how a jay cocks its
head to the left and to the right—

as if it is hearing the bugs crawl
or the earth cracking underneath it.
But here, in the place that is hiding
the power of infinitesimal beings and
light rapturous cavalcades of life,
when you see a small thing, you see it
in all of its worth. It shouts at
you to notice its depth and character.

Or, maybe it's just that I have slowed
down a bit and can actually see, again.

DISCUSSION

It often takes days, even weeks to arrive at a place of wonder and awe at the face of God in nature. Regardless of where we begin our spiritual journey, we must at some time and in some place come to the ground of seeing God in all that is. Seeing God in all that exists is the process of "remembering God' (called *"mneme theou"* by Eastern Christians). Remembering God is what the Koran was getting at in the quote, "All is perishing except His face".

Some people want to call this notion pantheism, even panentheism. The conversation is much deeper than this glib attempt to wall out truth. We are talking about the unabashed annihilation of the mystics—union with God. The Sufis call it "fana"—being destroyed in the face of supreme love.

Nature is so "not us", so OTHER, it is often easy to begin with it and try to find God in humanity after leaning how to see His face in nature. The startling vividness in the wilds of this earth-place paint broad strokes for us to see and sense; helping us to learn to notice. Nature is often a first step in self-disclosure.

The noticeable changes of spring and fall tend to call out to people because they are so large and visible. The changing of the leaves, the blooming of a wildflower—these things are fresh and identifiable against the backdrop of the summer green we have become accustomed to or the winter barrenness. These changes are highlighted by what they stand in contrast to.

Once we have seen a broad stroke of change, and the shifting view of nature is in our sight and mind, we begin to notice smaller things that match this theme. While we may first be pulled out of the slumber of our mundane routines by the fire red of the sassafras leaves in late September, our senses—hungry for more—may begin to notice the dying of the ferns, the abundance of falling nut casings or the subtle change in air and light as autumn is creeping in.

Taking note of the things that start an inner shift is important. These things occur year on year on year as we pass through time. We build up a whole database of wonder. We are storing memories of not only sights and sensory information, but we are shifting from survival in the world, to wonder at the world. We move from commonness to beatific vision on the backs of these little changes.

Sometimes we simply need these changes to lift our head up from staring at the ground and the path which we trod. All at once, we are awakened to take in the whole vista, not just our shoe hitting the dirt. And, when we do, something in us opens. We are aghast at the overwhelming mystery that is all around us. "Everything is perishing except His face."

Snowdrops and trout lilies do this for me every year. As they push out of the fallen leaf carpet on the forest floor, their greening stems, and tender flower blossoms pose visual contrast to the common brown I have lived with in the "colding" months. They make me stop. Soon I begin to search, with a flutter in my heart, for more flowers poking through.

As I go from plant to plant, a space opens in my heart. The space becomes filled with hope, newness, and wonder. I am amazed again, that life springs forth. Despite the droll and boring nature of routine deadness, there is something that slowly creeps in and opens me wide. It opens me to possibility, dreams, and grandeur. A tiny bud can open this great space.

We do not often sit back and review the powerful processes at work in our growing. The sense organs gather all sorts of input and relay it to the heart, and mind, and soul to sift through and interpret. This goes on, and on, and on all of the time. Stopping and recognizing this subterranean mill that is grinding the stuff of life into grist is an awesome contemplation in and of itself.

Where does the excitement come from when we see a clump of deer hair on a branch and realize a doe was here this morning? What feeling arises when we see a bird reach into the nest and feed its young with a worm just newly unearthed? When our eyes grow wide as a monster trout nuzzles in close to shore, what fills the heart?

These shifts and movements make all of the difference. It becomes the difference between starting the day with an unbelievably clear sense of lightness and peace or starting the day with the regular burden and chaos.

Once this process is uncovered, it becomes hard to feed on things that do not nourish. Once wonder sparks our being to life, we are never the same. Bliss creeps in and we learn to find it in smaller and smaller servings that will nourish us for longer and longer pieces of time. At some point, all of the great sages were able to gain sustenance from the raw energy that comes from watching a sunrise, a leaf fall on the pond, or the brilliance of the moon.

We capture the moment. Take it in. We nurse our being on every drop of nectar it has to provide.

GLEANINGS

Pearls of Wisdom we have found in this poem

- ❖ Trout lilies call forth awe
- ❖ We can miss small changes
- ❖ We become accustomed to things around us
- ❖ Becoming accustomed to things often robs us of awakening moments
- ❖ Animals can give us pause
- ❖
- ❖
- ❖
- ❖
- ❖
- ❖
- ❖
- ❖
- ❖
- ❖
- ❖
- ❖
- ❖

INSIGHTS

What leaps out at you from the poem:

What descriptive words do you like or identify with:

What colors, moods, or emotions do you hear in the poem:

What spiritual value or trait do you overhear in these words:

How does the HOLY ONE fit into this imagery or notion:

BRIDGES, PATHS, AND WATERS; DIRT, SKY, AND MOUNTAINS

How would you change or enrich the poem:

Write your own poem or paragraph of prose to encapsulate similar ideas:

How does the HOLY ONE speak to you through these ideas:

How do you feel your life being called to change:

Is there someone you feel would connect with the ideas in this poem:

Pretend you were writing to that person (above), how would you describe what you have learned or felt to them:

90 BRIDGES, PATHS, AND WATERS; DIRT, SKY, AND MOUNTAINS

Draw this poem:

How does this connect you to awe, wonder, or radical amazement:

10

POEM

"Sad Oak"

I have stood here
for decades, for centuries.
I have felt that river wrap
her arms around my roots,
around this dirt
and then recoil—curving
and cutting in straight and
crooked lines.

I have watched her children
come and go. I have watched
the First People—the Lenapi -
plant fish from her banks and feed
off the wild berries that push up
on her shores. I have watched
the General and his men push
off from her edges and travel
by night to surprise their own
countrymen—foreigners all of them.
I have watched the farmers take
silt from her banks to till into
their crops, learning the craft
of fish planting from the naked ones.
I have watched the new ones
dump hot colored liquid into
her blood and make her cringe -

giving up her harvest of fish. I
have watched these new ones
tame her and prod her with
concrete and asphalt, thinking
they could persuade her from
the rising she does with such pleasure
and rhythm. I have watched
as the people have forgotten to
make offerings to her—asking
her blessing; forgetting to enter
her with love and abandon.

The turkeys, they have pulled back.
The deer have all but stopped coming.
The naked ones are gone altogether.
What will happen to her?
Of late, she does not smile
when I throw my acorns to her and
drop my leaves on her. She used to
laugh when I tickled her with my
colored and dying hair. Now she is silent
and I fear for what will come next.

My roots—my own roots—who have
clung so simply to the dirt that is
her banks, have soured. Pieces of
me die as I drink her poisoned draught.
I am dying from her, from the one
who has been my life, my sweetness,
my health. I am dying from her waters.

That she does not talk to me
has made me sad. Where has she gone?
What has become of my thunderously
tender Delaware? Why does she
get so very bone dry? Why does
she not laugh as she lifts the debris
of life, carrying it to another place,

to another people?
I miss this woman, so strong
and so soft. I miss the caresses
she gave me. Her silence has
deafened me and I do not
care if I go on to see another people.
I do not care if I grow another limb.

Her silence has made me still. And,
it is not the stillness I enjoyed after our
sister wind had forced me to swing and
dance and clamber. It is the stillness
of being ill.

I have watched so much. I have
watched too much. I too must grow
silent, grow still, grow sick
and die. My time has come and
I am sad. I do still hope
that the naked ones will return. I do
still hope that someone gains their wits
and cleans up her banks and makes her
waters pure to drink—again.

DISCUSSION

It amazes me that there are so many communities in the natural world. We are often oblivious to the connectedness and interconnectedness of the web of all life because we function in our own world—willy-nilly to the natural world. However, the trees depend on the rivers, the dirt, and the air for their life. All of the wild is interlaced with one another.

I think of the powerful oaks that rise along the Delaware River. Some of them, at the place where Washington crossed the river may have actually seen the event. Regardless of whether they have or not, one thing is sure, trees, dirt, rocks, water, and air have all seen much more of the history of our planet—of the universe—than we have or ever will.

The trees along the river have taken to dying because of the pollution pushed up on her shores. They no longer taste the fresh, cold, clean draughts of refreshing water they once knew. Many will not live to tell their song in the blowing rattle of their leaves in the fall winds.

I wonder if the trees could talk to us in our words if they would tell us the Indians were kinder to them than we are. Would they know how we could rectify the scars of climate change? Would they tell us of their suffering at the experience of carbon emissions?

In the lifetime of the Delaware River, people have changed the way they live hundreds of times. People no longer build earth-wise homes and travel across her back non-invasively. We leave semi permanent structures on her banks and leave petroleum residue across her surfaces from our loud machines.

Part of the awe and reverence that we feel in the presence of the mystery of creation should leave us feeling accountable and responsible for her care. We should feel so connected to the grand and radical wonder we have before us that we would see all creation as a living, sentient being.

Yet we are so wrapped up in the worlds that we have made for ourselves that we see creation's need as less than our own. We see no way to disentangle ourselves from the long list of conveniences we have developed solely to make our own lives easier and allegedly more abundant. There is the rub. Can they really be more abundant if we are destroying the very beauty and grandeur that nourishes and sustains us?

I fear we have traded in on a lie that we ourselves have made, announced, and subsequently come to believe. It feels as if the mark of our own sinfulness reaches into our inability to stop the madness we have spawned and keeps us from caring for creation.

When we shut out awe, wonder, and radical amazement, we are keeping ourselves numb and distant from the very chords of interconnection that unite us with all creation. When we do not acknowledge the subconscious feeling of oneness, we are able to seek our own needs at the expense of others—now and in all time.

Nature clearly needs for us to act wisely. Scripture clearly teaches there can be no wisdom without awe—without the fear that lets us see our own small place in things.

We should be able to make the leap that asserts we need to care for creation—if not because we are woven into it, then because without it we will perish. Either of these propositions can help us radically re-arrange the way we live on the earth that is our home, and our matrix of life.

GLEANINGS

Pearls of Wisdom we have found in this poem

- ❖ Trees roots wrap around the earth
- ❖ Trees are nourished by rivers
- ❖ Nature interacts with itself
- ❖ All creation is interdependent
- ❖ nature looks to us for relationship
- ❖
- ❖
- ❖
- ❖
- ❖
- ❖
- ❖
- ❖
- ❖
- ❖
- ❖
- ❖
- ❖

INSIGHTS

What leaps out at you from the poem:

What descriptive words do you like or identify with:

What colors, moods, or emotions do you hear in the poem:

What spiritual value or trait do you overhear in these words:

How does the HOLY ONE fit into this imagery or notion:

How would you change or enrich the poem:

Write your own poem or paragraph of prose to encapsulate similar ideas:

How does the HOLY ONE speak to you through these ideas:

How do you feel your life being called to change:

Is there someone you feel would connect with the ideas in this poem:

100 BRIDGES, PATHS, AND WATERS; DIRT, SKY, AND MOUNTAINS

Pretend you were writing to that person (above), how would you describe what you have learned or felt to them:

Draw this poem:

How does this connect you to awe, wonder, or radical amazement:

11

POEM

"Alluvial Fans"

Fans spread out at
the base of the hills-
the base of our days-
escarping debris
deposited over time.

The force –
always down
hauls all sorts of silt
from the face of the
highlands to the foot
of the lowlands

Down,
always down falls
all that has died,
all that has decayed
and lost its grip.
It falls and is
washed away.
Are the things we
love really lost or
are they moved –
down, always down –
away to the pit

of our erosion.

Those pieces that have
washed away –
our youth,
our trust,
our freedom to be naïve.
Are they gone or
simply out of sight –
reaching out from
the basin of our days.

The nutrients and minerals
from the mountain
seed the basin
in a downward rush.
The mountains and
the hills laid low—a time
cast collaboration of the
prophets and erosion;
everything leveled.

Fingers of the mountain
stretch out
hoping to pull her along
the earth,
to widen her presence
along the surface. We
grow like this. All that runs
off of us produces chains
and foothills. Our life
touches another by the
build up of silt and alluvial
wear. It moves away from
our core. Then, lifetimes
later, the foothills of our
days spawn foothills and
are themselves carried away.

All things become one
as the work of time
spreads out the mountains,
bringing them all to the ground,
to the earth from which
they came.

The mountains and the hills
laid low.

DISCUSSION

I love how things move around in our lives. Things that were important to us in our youth may feel less important to us, but still hold some esteemed place in the landscape of our days. These things are not gone from our reality, only slightly altered.

Although the process of erosion in our lives feels as if it carries things out of our lives, it does not. Instead, we may need to shift our image and recognize that things may be moved a bit further away from center, but they are still there.

Look around you at the hills and the mountains. Particles of the earth—pieces of the dirt—are washed downward on them with every rain. Pieces that start at the top of the mountain are pulled down its slopes to form a new hill, a smaller hill that is built up over time.

The joy I had as a child raising a rabbit was something I thought I would never get back. In later years, working with troubled youth I was given the opportunity again to plug into the piece of me that loves rabbits. My wife and I raised over 30 rabbits with the children of the children's home. Then, when we had boys of our own, my wife and I raised at least another dozen rabbits.

I love their thoughtfulness. The way a rabbit sits, sniffing and sensing all that is around it: trying to feel danger and safety; sensing warmth and cold; smelling bees and flowers. It collects things from all around. It brings those things inside and then it knows how to respond.

I thought I had lost the ability to connect with the discernment rabbits teach. It all reappears—again and again—in my life. Each time it re-appeared it seemed a more aged and wise piece of my being. It settled into me better with each approach.

It is this way with other things. Peace and patience may be taken away from us, (moved down the hill a bit) only to be rediscovered again later. People move in and out of our lives; over and over again.

Just like the mountains, just like the hills, the geography of our lives is fluid. And, although things seem to escape us, they have not. They have simply been moved beyond our current view of things. They are moved beyond what we are willing to accept as our place. Perhaps we are larger than we let on.

One of the disadvantages of only living a few decades on this earth is that we do not get to see the full shape of how things are. Just like the river bending, we do not get to see all of the changes that are yet to come or that have already taken place. Our gift is imagination. We, like the rabbit can pick up clues and take in signs. We can figure them out and hold onto what we have pieced together, making maps of reality—drawings of the landscape.

The notion of illusion that this gives birth to in our lives is immense. We are not able to know truth unless we can capture its presence over time. We have to see how all of the things fit together, not just in one slice of our lives, but in the fullness of our lives if we are to ascertain the truth of those things. We can not know the depth of our relationships unless we weld together all of the fragments that they are made of—not in just one instance, but in all instances.

Like the earth, the mountains, and the hills, then, we are always growing in motion. We are expanding in time. What is today is only a piece of the whole. The illusion of life is that this one thing we hold is only what it is now. The myth is that what we are today is all that we are. Instead, we are spreading out from the moment we take form. It is not just the physical, tangible pieces of our lives that shift and grow. Our minds, and hearts, and souls that move out from their center, too.

The things that we connected with in childhood are still a part of our lives. The decisions we made as young adults still affect what we do today. The people that have nurtured us, fed us, and given us freedom are all still in there. So too are the moments of pain and suffering. The scars and injuries go with us.

Grace is not that the sufferings are taken away, but that we grow despite and because of them. These things are always present so we can make more informed choices; may act in ways that we know to be better. The collection of all of the pieces of our lives may give us a fuller view, if we will but acknowledge that they are not gone, that they have not vanished.

I find myself staring at these foothills, these fans from the mountain. They somehow feed me. They paint an image of my life for me. I can feel that image within, but I am less apt to make sense of it without these sisters of the dirt. Without these fingers reaching down from the mountain, down from the heights, I do not know what it is I feel.

GLEANINGS

Pearls of Wisdom we have found in this poem

- ❖ Mountains erode
- ❖ The debris washed down from mountains forms foothills
- ❖ Things are moved around in our lives
- ❖ Time carries things away
- ❖ The things carried away from us act as nourishment for others and other times
- ❖
- ❖
- ❖
- ❖
- ❖
- ❖
- ❖
- ❖
- ❖
- ❖
- ❖
- ❖

INSIGHTS

What leaps out at you from the poem:

What descriptive words do you like or identify with:

What colors, moods, or emotions do you hear in the poem:

What spiritual value or trait do you overhear in these words:

How does the HOLY ONE fit into this imagery or notion:

How would you change or enrich the poem:

Write your own poem or paragraph of prose to encapsulate similar ideas:

How does the HOLY ONE speak to you through these ideas:

How do you feel your life being called to change:

Is there someone you feel would connect with the ideas in this poem:

Pretend you were writing to that person (above), how would you describe what you have learned or felt to them:

BRIDGES, PATHS, AND WATERS; DIRT, SKY, AND MOUNTAINS

Draw this poem:

How does this connect you to awe, wonder, or radical amazement:

12

POEM

"Strata"

Our days are made of
varied ages and
altering composition.
Layers of change through
out time and space.

To feel the changes
that have been made
does not require
the minds' knowing alone—of where
one thing ends and
another begins.

Nor is the
heart's feeling enough.
We need a gut that senses change.

An intuition that
senses the shifting
plates and layers
of life. We need a
heart and a mind that will trust
the gut.

In us,
down deep and beneath
are movements we cannot see,
upheavals we will never see,
shifts we cannot know will come.

We can sense them.
We can lean forward at
the first stirrings—bend into
them and suppose or
hunch.

It is the gut that notices
this larger terrain—this immense
sliding. It is the gut that
feels its way through changing
landscape.

The eye may not see, the mind,
it may not know, the heart may
not feel, but the gut senses.
The gut holds on
to shudders and rumbles. The
gut explores valleys and
hills, the faults and
plates of the
topology of our lives.

The gut knows nothing
of fur and feathers,
of brocade and silk.
It holds no hope in the fine
and the soft: amid
the smooth and refined.

The heart and the mind, they
loll themselves to sleep
in the finery. Casting their

eyes on the silt and lace
of low grade terrain;
feeling for a faint
interior pulse that they
cannot know.

Our days shift and move
without regard for the mind's
vigilant hope for reason, and
the heart's need for rhythm
and rhyme. Things
move about without warning.
I cannot hope to see
that plate raised up above the others
or that one dropped down below.
The gut knows disturbance:
turbulence is its language –
and it knows it well.

My gut feels them:
A jarring drop or jolting
rise is measured for sure in
the gut. The heart, the heart
reaches out and feels
through the layers of space
and time for the shifting
and the rolling forces
We no longer see—the
sorrow and the joy
that arrives from change
ushered in on the current
of the hummingbird's wing
at noon day.

Layers of life
that we cannot see.

We are piles of layers
within the twist of time
and the stretch of space;
the spray of the wave
and the stir of air.
We hold on amid
our lack of ingenuity;
we dream on despite our
innocence of any true power.
Sensing only the dark,
feeling only the layers
of our piled past,
we hope against hell that our
heart and our mind have
listened well and found
what is true, what is sure –
what the gut has to offer.

DISCUSSION

Our lives are made of layers. One on top of another, they do not always meld or mend themselves together. They exist almost as tectonic plates, slipping and sliding on occasion, causing rumbles and grumbles to be heard and felt above.

I love the earthiness of this image. There is a real sense of the subconscious and even the un-conscious when we pick up language like this. Many folks do not take a lot of stock in the movements that come from deep within, many don't even sense them. Not sensing them or to not taking stock in them does not diminish their reality or presence.

A simple pragmatic way to look at these layers is simply to acknowledge that every experience, emotion, action, thought and desire we have had or have interacted with is a part of a large collection of stuff that exist (somewhere) within.

The Buddhists speak about the idea of "field consciousness" and relate it to planting and watering seeds that have been taken from existing plants. We have this great big expansive field of being. We can harvest and plant seeds from anyone else's experience and even from pieces of our own experience. We simply must select the seeds we wish to plant, we must plant them, we must water them, and we must watch them grow toward harvest.

I like this notion. Gardens are vital for the nurturance and healing of both soul and body. Seeing life as a field is pleasing. We can choose seeds from Jesus, or from our parents, or from that class we attended. We can plant them, take care of them, and then watch these experiences, emotions, actions, thoughts, and desires grow into an abundant harvest.

Think of it. We choose how we will respond to our children when they bring us news we do not want to hear. At that moment, we have the choice of planting and watering seeds of compassion or seeds of anger. We are planting more things in the field with every moment of life. This occurs even if we do not acknowledge what is happening. Imagine the focus we could gain if we did acknowledge it.

The idea of layers to life functions the same. We have phases and groupings of responses to life all built up in our lives today. There are the layers of our lives that represent the teachings of the Gospels. There are the layers of our lives represent our family's ideologies. We have the layers of our lives that represent all our past actions at work; or home, or school, or church. All of these layers are in there—in us—making up whom we are and have become.

Movement and upheaval is sure to come. They exist in every life. Often they come in waves or cycles. We often become poised and ready for the next one to occur: a parent is hospitalized, a spouse loses a job, or a child fails a class. All of our interior layers begin moving and shifting.

In times of crisis and immense activity, we are sometimes surprised by seeing a piece of our lives—hidden for some time—become present and demand attention. These moments remind us of how complex we really are. A parent goes into the hospital and helplessness emerges. We feel a need to pray again. We get protective with our children. These arise from deeper places in the layers of our days; places we may have forgotten existed.

There does not have to be a crisis in order to have things percolate up from the depths within. When we repeat an experience or a situation from our past, the familiarity causes a disturbance within. I moved back to a camp I had attended 34 years ago in order to take a fulltime job there. Sometimes just hiking to a spot on the property takes me back thirty odd years and I relive some ancient value or activity.

Most of these shifts are not something we can immediately put word or even feeling to. They start as an impression or image in the gut. We sense something has changed or shifted. It takes some stillness to plug into these signs and signals and find out what they are attached to. We often write them off as nothing. We sometimes say, "That makes me feel old", or "WOW, I haven't thought about that for a long time." These are signs that we sense movement.

Most of us have never given much thought to the anthropology of our spiritual lives. We have a mind that thinks, reasons, and remembers. We have a heart that feels. We have a soul or gut that longs and desires. These are all different layers to our existence and our way of being. Acknowledging these unique functions is a way of looking at the distinctly different apparatus of the interior life.

Spending time recognizing that these three are all at work in everything we do can help us discover pieces we do not see. We have thoughts about our jobs, feelings about our jobs, and also longings and desires about our jobs. Each of these is a slightly different aspect of our way of holding the notion of "our jobs" within. Very close and sometimes overlapping in their responses, they are individual, nonetheless. They form the topography of our lives; the landscape of our being.

The gut in this poem does not deal with the finer things of life, the things that lull it into the narcissism of abundance. We can get carried away with feelings and thoughts, but impressions are not something we tend to obsess on. Our gut is more concerned about keeping us alive.

Paul MacLean spent time discussing the three aspects of the brain. His model is referred to as the triune brain. He talks about the central core of the limbic brain, the wrapping around that as the cerebellum, and the wrapping around that as the neo-cortex.

Each layer or sheath handles higher functioning levels. The limbic brain is referred to as the reptilian brain. It is responsible for survival mechanisms. The cerebellum is the mammalian brain and handles social/bonding issues. The neo-cortex handles integrative functioning that occurs between left-brain, right-brain and the other two brains: limbic and cerebellum. The neo-cortex is also what makes us able to move, develop, and become as individuals—the sense of "I AM" comes from this part of the brain.

It does not take long to see the soul, the heart and the mind unfolding in these brain terms. Call them desiring, feeling and thinking, if you will. It is just as easy to plug in Freudian or Jungian concepts to the model.

The neo-cortex is the least understood, and is in the infancy of our ability to use it as a tool expressing the full range of capabilities in the human brain-system. While certain thinking and analyzing functions may occur here it, is the ability to observe thought, feeling, and drives that is the quintessential prize of having this mass of cells and functions in our bodies.

Poetry is one of the many arenas in which we can find all three functions at play in one notion. The gut senses images out there in the outside world, connects with them and begins to add layers of feeling and thought to expression of words on the page. It is not unusual to go back to a poem, or piece of art, years after enfleshing it and see in it a raw and deep complexity that you had know idea was present when it was created. This ability to see development and interior ingenuity is a function of our higher thinking.

GLEANINGS

Pearls of Wisdom we have found in this poem

- ❖ There are intricate layers to life
- ❖ There is a depth in people
- ❖ The mind thinks
- ❖ The heart feels
- ❖ The gut senses
- ❖
- ❖
- ❖
- ❖
- ❖
- ❖
- ❖
- ❖
- ❖
- ❖
- ❖
- ❖
- ❖

INSIGHTS

What leaps out at you from the poem:

What descriptive words do you like or identify with:

What colors, moods, or emotions do you hear in the poem:

What spiritual value or trait do you overhear in these words:

How does the HOLY ONE fit into this imagery or notion:

How would you change or enrich the poem:

Write your own poem or paragraph of prose to encapsulate similar ideas:

How does the HOLY ONE speak to you through these ideas:

How do you feel your life being called to change:

Is there someone you feel would connect with the ideas in this poem:

Pretend you were writing to that person (above), how would you describe what you have learned or felt to them:

Draw this poem:

How does this connect you to awe, wonder, or radical amazement:

13

POEM

"Escarpment"

Some things wear you down;
a deep aging in your center,
an erosion of your soul
or maybe your heart.

It does not kill you,
but
it lays you bare,
open,
exposed.

This wearing down becomes clear
in the middle of life. One thing
comes along: a death, an accident,
a final straw that lights the mind's
sky, and all at once you
see what has been there all along -
that which has undone you—that
which has worn you away.

There it is.
And,
don't be shy,
it goes
against your earliest hopes, your
youthful ideals, and your grandest

theories. There it is,
a piece of you, one
that was left exposed
as if it were something new.

Like the rock held deep
in the earth, erosion,
time,
alterations pull the dirt
from all around the stone.
They pull the dirt
from this piece of you
they move the pebbles from
your side, they move the sand from behind
and you are revealed
by the violence of change.

This need not be horrid violence -
the great unleashing slide of
the glacier as it tears away from it's
century nest,
pushing
with a crashing speed.

A simple negotiated shift
is enough. A slow movement
back and forth, to and fro,
earth and weather,
drifting and decaying and
just simply washing away.

Some things wear you down;
a deep aging in your center,
an erosion of your soul
or maybe your heart.

DISCUSSION

Life has an eroding process to it. The whole nature of time seems to remove things from us, take them away from us. While they may still be within close proximity, erosion makes them feel as if they are removed forever from the landscape of our days.

In middle-life, if not before, a tiredness arises from having to tend to the many fingers of our lives, the many facets of our days among others on this earth. We are deeply connected, because we have learned from the earlier phases of our life that connecting with people and the processes of life is vital and increases the integrity we so long to develop and hold onto. And yet, all of this devotion to integrity wears us out.

We start to notice small changes in who we are and perhaps in some of the decisions we have made. We feel the weight of compromise as a bit heavy and we wonder if all of the small compromises we have made in order to navigate and negotiate the thousand and one tendrils of life have been worth it or even necessary.

When you see an escarpment on a hill, a place that suddenly drops off with a clear marking of eroded earth just below, you can sense the feel of loss and change in your life. Seeing the slides of rocks as they approach the drop reminds you of the times you have scurried against all odds to climb back to a safe place in life—a place of security and sure footing where you can find rest and shelter.

You can feel the eroding of life. It leaves you feeling bare and exposed. You feel open and vulnerable to things. In youth, many of the same processes occur but bravado tends to keep us feeling like we have the edge, as if we are still in charge. Aging teaches us that there is an illusion in the thinking that we are always capable of keeping things from sliding away, being pulled out of place.

It only takes that one hospitalization of a close loved one to put it in perspective. We have a need to tend to them, but we have "all of this other stuff" that we still have to deal with. We have our lives, our jobs, our children, our spouses to look after and tend to on a daily basis. Although we may be able to run on life's fumes and take care of all of these things, one hospitalization comes along and topples the scales. Alternatively, perhaps it is two or three emergency situations that land on our doorstep all at once.

We tend to know, in some deep place, that these landslides will not kill us. At the same time, we sense that things are changing. The earth that we have been rooted in until this moment has given up soil and our hold on it is somehow lessened. We feel we may not be able to hold on the same. We can feel support being taken from us, pulled down the hill, to the drop off.

Some notice these changes with sadness; feeling a hollowness within. When will the healing come? How will we find stability in the movement? From whence is our help to come? It comes in small ways.

A friend—who has been through the same shift—will say one small thing that will remind you that there is hope; that you have been through all of this before. You will look out one day and notice the things you thought you had lost are not gone, just moved further along—perhaps just out of place. You will seek some help from outside yourself and that seeking will enable you find an answer, gain a little perspective, or give you enough distance to recuperate.

Ultimately, one either comes to the awakening that this is life; we encounter changes and we become new beings, new creatures; or, one insists that we must always remain the same—we have got to get back what we have lost—and becomes bitter when this cannot or does not happen. Noticing the beauty of these natural displays of loss and shifting earth can free us up to come to peace with the many alterations that lie just out of our grasp, but still within our lives.

Being vulnerable is not an end. We do not have to fall apart because we are weak. Moments of shifting earth provide opportunities for roots to grow deeper into the soil that is changing on the surface. A gnarly root, above the ground, is a testimony of the will to survive and a thing of beauty to others who have been in touch with their human suffering.

All of this shifting and, all of this sliding can actually help us to find that still point within. We can find the portion of our life that is our core. People open up to the awareness that the eroding details of life are not who we are. We are not those things. There is an interior self that is beyond all of the sliding and washing away.

We can not find this without first looking at the prevailing changes that are the stuff of life. If we cannot first acknowledge that erosion is a part of our days, then we will never be able to move to a place that sees awe, wonder, or amazement in viewing what the erosion produces. We cannot move on to see that it is not our core that erodes; it is simply the earthy stuff of our days on this planet that shifts.

GLEANINGS

Pearls of Wisdom we have found in this poem

- ❖ Things move and shift
- ❖ The earth slides and erodes
- ❖ Time, gravity, and erosion pulls things down, pulls things away
- ❖ We feel exposed when things shift
- ❖ Our youthful bravado may not be a deep feeling
- ❖
- ❖
- ❖
- ❖
- ❖
- ❖
- ❖
- ❖
- ❖
- ❖
- ❖
- ❖

INSIGHTS

What leaps out at you from the poem:

What descriptive words do you like or identify with:

What colors, moods, or emotions do you hear in the poem:

What spiritual value or trait do you overhear in these words:

How does the HOLY ONE fit into this imagery or notion:

How would you change or enrich the poem:

Write your own poem or paragraph of prose to encapsulate similar ideas:

How does the HOLY ONE speak to you through these ideas:

How do you feel your life being called to change:

Is there someone you feel would connect with the ideas in this poem:

Pretend you were writing to that person (above), how would you describe what you have learned or felt to them:

Draw this poem:

How does this connect you to awe, wonder, or radical amazement:

14

POEM

"High Rocks"

The earth is
held together
up here with
cedar roots,
with hickory roots
and the constant hope
of no rain.

The red-shale soil
loves to wash
itself,
down,
down
to the ravine below
becoming silt for the Tohickon Creek -
down to the Indian's "Deer-bone Creek".

The dirt is
made up here
with the slipping
and the sliding of rock;
on rock;
stone against stone
and rain on earth.

The pounding and the force
makes dirt of the stone.

Creeping along in
the fingers of the rain
the dirt is grabbed,
the dirt is pushed
along the roots that cling
tightly to life
and to the vertical growth.

The earth is
held together up here,
by cedar roots,
by hickory roots,
and the constant hope
of no rain.

DISCUSSION

Much of the time, we do not see the holding on that trees do. The root structures lie below the surface, just beyond our sight. We know in side that trees hold tight to the earth, that the dirt gives them support. When we see roots seeming to hang on for dear life, it makes an impression.

Hiking in river and stream basins, along eroded hills and knobs, I have seen trees clutching amid the downward falling of dirt and stone. It seems escarpments are luring trees to their demise. There is a clear sense of conflict happening when these two forces meet.

The one force is trying above all odds to survive and grow. Hungering and thirsting for nutrients and water the tree holds fast.

The other force is prying all things away from where they are. Beckoning and calling for all things to wash away in wind and rain.

When we see these sorts of odds playing out in the human community, we tend to assign value and moral implication to what we observe. If the poor are being oppressed, we see this as wrong. If the state requires immense taxation of its members, we see this as unfair.

I think we step away from platitudes when we see nature at play. What my heart acknowledges in seeing a tree on a cliff losing the very dirt it clings too is not that the dirt or the rain and wind are bad. What it feels is the pain of living among many forces. If we superimpose anything on the scenes it is a sense of "what we must do" to stop this thing from occurring. How have we failed?

I am not suggesting that this is right or wrong. That would be out of step. What I am suggesting is that there seems to be a raw feeling in seeing nature. This raw feeling—for a split second—is nothing more than a noticing. We see and we take it in; our hearts assess and make an impression on us of the conflict afoot. Just as this split second passes, we move into the next thing. Perhaps it is a feeling of how "sad" this appears. Perhaps it is a feeling of our "need" to interact and save.

It is that split second when nature is most aptly our teacher. What we gain from viewing creation all around us is a series of impressions that become the backdrop of our interpretive lives.

Some people are prone to interpreting through the eyes of fear. How will this affect us? Are we safe from these things? Should we be here? Some are prone to interpreting through the eyes of love. How grand this scene is. This is a wonder beyond my imagining. This is the depth of life. These eyes may also be called the eyes of separateness and the eyes of unity.

For those who see themselves over and against nature—as separate—there may be a tendency to proclaim how we are different, to judge, to repair, and to fix. Those who see themselves as part of nature are often left to being able to feel their place in the midst of it. I think that is the crux of what we have been observing.

Awe, wonder, and radical amazement are all states of being. They are ways the heart may be with experiences, in this case of nature and creation. When we choose to be in awe—for in many cases we must train ourselves to enter this state (although some immense natural scenes call it out of us)—we are in a state in which our mind somehow just drops into our hearts. We go from seeing into feeling with little notice.

I think of the many opportunities I have had to sit with nature amid personal crisis and turmoil. In those moments, I do not feel a connection with the wild. I feel like a lonely soul, in pain amid the beauty of the woods. But, as I sit, the encounter has a way of seeping into me and challenging me to open, to just be; not to feel my pain in the woods, but just to be still in the woods without any mention of my pain, suffering, or separateness of being. Then, as I notice my presence in this experience, as I shift into the impressions of my heart, this peace becomes curative and healing.

It is in these moments that I am cracked open. So it is with nature. We must force ourselves to be out among her to have experiences that are larger than we are. We cannot gain from simply showing up on occasion. We must take ourselves to these scenes of beauty and we must do it over and over again so we can begin to recognize how awe, wonder, and radical amazement transform us.

Although we may instantly acknowledge awe when we see a breathtaking vista, we must train ourselves to go often to the awe in time and space so we may be transformed by it. Too much of our contemporary life is among the things we have made ourselves. It may be gadgets, or groups, or systems, or projects but they are all our own toys and devices. Escaping from the world of "us" is vital human nutrient that we all need.

We could go around the discussion all day, "What drives us to having an experience of awe? Is it planned, or is it spontaneous?" If we do not place ourselves in situations to "be with" the awesome song of creation, then it will not matter what we believe. Our musings here are mute without placing ourselves in front of what God has called forth.

It does not matter—for this path of growth—whether the tree makes a sound when it falls with or without people watching. What matters is that we get ourselves to the trees. There is healing and nourishment that comes from being with trees, these sisters of creation. There are whole layers of our lives that are touched and opened—places that make us more whole as people—when we are out among the wild places of this earth.

These places change us. They change us deeply.

The action of the conflict between the rain and the earth is what produces the wet vehicle by which the red silt slides over the rocks and eventually makes its way to the creek basin below. The action of the conflict between rock and rock is what produces the red shale dust that is waiting for the rain to take it away. These conflicts, these actions are the same in our lives. What is it that carries us away? What is it that wears us down to dust?

The trees hold on, as do we. What holds the earth of our lives together is no less awesome. Against all odds of entropy, there are daily maneuvers that save our lives. Small desires to persevere and hang on are noble measures—things of beauty. The daily act of living produces pieces of us that will wash away and join the greater stream of life on earth. The quality of that runoff is made in and by our hearts.

GLEANINGS

Pearls of Wisdom we have found in this poem

- ❖ Trees hang on to the earth
- ❖ Dirt is produced from nature's friction
- ❖ Conflict is a part of all life
- ❖ Beauty moves us into our heart
- ❖ What is washed away joins others somehow
- ❖
- ❖
- ❖
- ❖
- ❖
- ❖
- ❖
- ❖
- ❖
- ❖
- ❖
- ❖
- ❖

INSIGHTS

What leaps out at you from the poem:

What descriptive words do you like or identify with:

What colors, moods, or emotions do you hear in the poem:

What spiritual value or trait do you overhear in these words:

How does the HOLY ONE fit into this imagery or notion:

144 BRIDGES, PATHS, AND WATERS; DIRT, SKY, AND MOUNTAINS

How would you change or enrich the poem:

Write your own poem or paragraph of prose to encapsulate similar ideas:

How does the HOLY ONE speak to you through these ideas:

How do you feel your life being called to change:

Is there someone you feel would connect with the ideas in this poem:

Pretend you were writing to that person (above), how would you describe what you have learned or felt to them:

BRIDGES, PATHS, AND WATERS; DIRT, SKY, AND MOUNTAINS

Draw this poem:

How does this connect you to awe, wonder, or radical amazement:

15

POEM

"Roots"

They start so quietly
here,
slipping from the trunk,
descending into dirt
and mud.
There is barely a whisper
where the roots pull away
from each other,
where the roots pull
away from the trunk
and plunge
into the earth.
I wish I knew how deep
they went;
what they look like
down under
the soil;
what they do there.
But I must tear them up
to find that out. I must
give them over to death.
Some men would,
but I cannot.

Until I die,
great hickory brother,
I will wish in the
shadow of your
whispered roots. I
will wish and imagine
and make stories of
your life underground.

DISCUSSION

Trees hold on to earth. They do this through their roots. What is a trunk one minute turns into a root the next, and is buried and gone below the surface of the earth. We cannot see their climb into the dirt but we know it is drinking up stuff that will add new growth and produce new life for the tree not only today, but in the future as well..

I think of the thousand and one things I am rooted in, that hold me fast. There is God, my family, my work, the communities of my life, the sights, the sounds, the tastes, the smells, and the feeling of everything all around. A whirling, swirling mass of time and space experiences of being hold me in place.

Like the roots of a tree, my nourishment happens out of the realm of my knowing quite often. My connection to Christ often feeds me when I encounter various trials or conflicts in my life. Holding my wife's hand or touching my son's face carries nutrients in to me that change me and add new life. I am given hope by years of prayer, or singing, or being in communion with people. I may not see the correlation or the connection, but it exists and is active all the same.

At once life is both visible and explainable, and invisible and ineffable. We can make sense of some things and others are beyond our explaining.

Thomas Aquinas tells us whatever we can say about God is less accurate concerning who God is than if we would say nothing at all. It is the Taoist principle that naming something somehow lessens it. Giving word to experience is only a candle in the darkness. Feeling these things or connecting from the heart is where the deepest truth abides.

Where do we gain nourishment and stability? What holds us in place and feeds us? These questions follow us all of the days of our lives. We most often do not really know what is happening to us in life, what is setting up all of the feelings, emotions, thoughts and impressions we are having at any one moment. Checking around us for the ground we are rooted in can give us some clues.

I wonder in rapt mystery at how a tree can hold on in an immense rain and wind. I am startled by the strength that comes from something so brittle. I have often found pause watching how people survive and make it through the storms in their days on earth. A speechlessness prevails so as not to lessen what is so grand.

Being out here with the rocks and the trees, the wind and the rain, the lakes and paths and mountains opens me up to a greater mystery and beauty than my words can tell. A poem, although it gets at the truth of a thing, is clearly only a boat that is tossed aside on the shores, when I have arrived at the far banks of experience.

Deeper, always deeper go the roots of living things. Holding and feeding are a part of how all things survive. In most cases, a tree has to adapt to where it finds itself planted. It may send roots deeper to water that lies below, but it cannot pick itself up and move closer to the stream. It finds ways to cope.

We are given to mobility and have the ability to choose our rooting material and nutrient source. We can sidle up to times and places that feed us best. Finding those places and discovering those times tends to be the measure of our days on earth. We are creatures in search of a homeland. We wander amid the awe of creation. We swim through wonder. We are climbing in radical amazement.

GLEANINGS

Pearls of Wisdom we have found in this poem

- ❖ Trunks turn into roots
- ❖ Roots dig into the earth
- ❖ Trees search for survival with their roots
- ❖ Nourishment is critical for life
- ❖ We can find places and times to be rooted in
- ❖
- ❖
- ❖
- ❖
- ❖
- ❖
- ❖
- ❖
- ❖
- ❖
- ❖
- ❖
- ❖

Chapter 15   153

INSIGHTS

What leaps out at you from the poem:

What descriptive words do you like or identify with:

What colors, moods, or emotions do you hear in the poem:

What spiritual value or trait do you overhear in these words:

How does the HOLY ONE fit into this imagery or notion:

154 BRIDGES, PATHS, AND WATERS; DIRT, SKY, AND MOUNTAINS

How would you change or enrich the poem:

Write your own poem or paragraph of prose to encapsulate similar ideas:

How does the HOLY ONE speak to you through these ideas:

How do you feel your life being called to change:

Is there someone you feel would connect with the ideas in this poem:

Pretend you were writing to that person (above), how would you describe what you have learned or felt to them:

BRIDGES, PATHS, AND WATERS; DIRT, SKY, AND MOUNTAINS

Draw this poem:

How does this connect you to awe, wonder, or radical amazement:

www.ingramcontent.com/pod-product-compliance
Lightning Source LLC
Chambersburg PA
CBHW051102160426
43193CB00010B/1285